THE ROOTS OF

AMERICAN FOREIGN POLICY

THE ROOTS OF
AMERICAN
FOREIGN POLICY

*An Analysis of
Power and Purpose*

by Gabriel Kolko

BEACON PRESS : BOSTON

To the victims,
those who resist,
and to the future!

ACKNOWLEDGMENTS

MANY FRIENDS provoked and encouraged the writing of this volume, often without knowing it. They may not agree with all that follows, but because the book is in a sense a response to certain of their theses, they will understand that our disagreements on details do not obscure the more essential fact that we share the same values and goals. Their questions, arguments, and ideas clearly influenced the form of this book, and since I cannot absolve them of the aid I found most invaluable—and hence some measure of responsibility for what follows—I shall leave them unnamed and convey my appreciation directly.

I completed this volume while I was a visiting fellow at the Institute for Policy Studies, and I am most grateful for its support during 1967–68. Mr. John Rumbarger ably helped me during the summer of 1966 in the preparation of data on American leaders. I presented an earlier, longer version of the chapter on the United States and Vietnam to the International War Crimes Tribunal in Stockholm in May 1967.

As in the case of everything I have written, my wife, Joyce, has been of inestimable sustenance and help. Her role in making this book possible was very great.

GABRIEL KOLKO

CONTENTS

Introduction xi

1. *The Men of Power* 3

2. *The American Military and Civil Authority* 27

3. *The United States and World Economic Power* 48

4. *The United States in Vietnam, 1944–66* 88

Epilogue: On Reason and Radicalism 133

Notes 139

Index 160

INTRODUCTION

FOR A GROWING NUMBER OF AMERICANS the war in Vietnam has become the turning point in their perception of the nature of American foreign policy, the traumatizing event that requires them to look again at the very roots, assumptions, and structure of a policy that is profoundly destructive and dangerous. Vietnam is the logical outcome of a consistent reality we should have understood long before the United States applied much of its energies to ravaging one small nation.

We can only comprehend Vietnam in the larger context of the relations of the United States to the Third World, removing from our analytic framework superfluous notions of capriciousness, accident, and chance as the causal elements in American foreign and military policy. For the events in Vietnam expose in a sustained and systematic manner those American qualities that have led to one of the most frightful examples of barbarism of mechanized man against man known to modern history. The logical, deliberative aspects of American power at home and its interest abroad show how fully irrelevant are notions of accident and innocence in explaining the diverse applications of American power today, not only in Vietnam but throughout the

Third World. If America's task of repressing the irrepressible is doomed to failure because it is impossible for six percent of the world's population to police and control the globe, critics of American policy should not attribute the undertaking to omission or ignorance. For if the United States can impose its will on the recalcitrant revolutionaries everywhere it will gain immensely thereby, and its losses will be proportionately great if it fails.

★

To understand policy one must know the policy-makers—the men of power—and define their ideological view and their backgrounds. This means we must better perceive the nature of bureaucracy and state institutions in modern America, and determine whether such organizations carry with them distinctive economic and ideological attributes likely to emerge in the form of specific policies. It is, of course, the dominant fashion in the study of bureaucracy to ascribe to the structure of decision-making bureaucracy a neutral, independent rationale, and to drain away the class nature of formal institutions—indeed, to deny that men of power are something more than disinterested, perhaps misguided, public servants. The fact, of course, is that men of power do come from specific class and business backgrounds and ultimately have a very tangible material interest in the larger contours of policy. And although some are indeed seemingly perfect models of the neutral and disinterested public servant, both, in practice, implement the same policies.

We must confront anew the meaning of the concept of consensus or public opinion and the way it operates in the policy process. On one hand the seemingly shared beliefs, values, and consensus in society appear more critical than any single interest. But the fact that a ruling class makes its policies operate, even when the mass of society ceases to endorse them, and that the voluntaristic and occasionally enforced social goals benefit individuals rather than all of society, is a central reality most analysts perpetually exclude from a descriptive explanation of American society. That the voluntaristic basis of consensus usually justifies the actions of the men of power is less consequential than that, as we see today in the case of the American public and Vietnam, the policy continues when mass agreement withers away and even disappears. For consensus is identifiable with class goals and needs, suitably wrapped in a vague ideology of American nationalism and its global responsibility. These class goals and interests prevail even when the consensus disappears, and it is at this very point we see that administrators base policy on the control of power and interests rather than society's sanction or consent. I explore how and why this occurs in Chapter One.

In the chapter on American military and civil authority I have attempted to show how pervasive are the assumptions and power of those civilians who run Washington, and how they have freely utilized the Military Establishment as a tool for advancing their own interests rather than the mythical independent goals of the officers. For businessmen and their political cohorts have defined the limits within which the military formulates strategy, extending their values and definitions of priorities over essentially docile generals. A closer look at the nature of the military today only further reveals the pervasiveness of the business-defined consensus, as well as the institutional levers by which the men of power apply their resources and attain their ends. The details, of course, are found in Chapter Two, but suffice it to say the facts reinforce the point that not a mythical "military-industrial" complex but civilian authority and civilian-defined goals are the sources of American foreign and military policy—and the American malaise. To understand this essential fact is also to reject conspiratorial theories, as well as the liberals' common explanations of the origins of dangerous and destructive policies. It means that in evaluating the responsibility for these policies we must seriously take into account the role of today's respectables—the self-styled liberal realists and businessmen, in and out of the Administration, who are the architects of the decades-old premises for the conduct of American diplomacy. It requires, above all, a much clearer definition of the nature of American power and interest in the modern world, an assessment of who gains and loses as a result of the policies Washington pursues.

In my discussion of the United States and world economic power I undertake to outline more precisely the magnitude of American objectives and interests, especially as they lead to global interventionism and give some rational basis for understanding the following description of the United States in Vietnam. I offer this outline on the international economy as an example of the kinds of ingredients and data that must go into a comprehensive portrait of the world role of the United States today. Both critics and defenders of current policy have largely ignored these elements in debates over the motives of American conduct, but such explanations make sense of much that has occurred and is yet to come to pass. Moreover, it is in terms of the world economy that the business and economic backgrounds of the men of power become especially germane, for their perception of the world and United States objectives in it reflects their attempt to apply overseas the structural relations which fattened their interests at home. In brief, they see the role of the state as a servant and regulator of economic affairs, and given the integration of American capitalism with the world economy, particularly with the Third World, their use of the Military Establishment to attain their ends abroad is one of the primary causes of American conduct in the world today.

It is in this setting and with this leadership that the United States has attempted to interact with the Third World both economically and militarily. This painful and insecure relationship is in fact the most important single challenge to confront the United States since the end of the Second World War, and its resolution has defined the course of world politics in the past decades, just as it may limit it in those yet to follow. The American effort has assumed two forms: military and economic.

The military undertaking has, on the whole, failed. As I indicate in my discussion of the Military Establishment, until the end of the Eisenhower Administration an overwhelming concern for nuclear strategy forced the United States largely to ignore the far more critical guerrilla and peasant revolutionary movements that it could not reach with missiles or the American ideology. Vietnam was the first serious American effort to relate militarily to the dominant political and social probabilities of the remainder of this century: the graduation of the poor, neocolonial states to a dynamic stage of development via revolutionary nationalist movements dedicated to combating stagnation and misery. This American encroachment into Vietnam took, as I maintain in the last chapter, the character of an international intervention rather than, as is commonly suggested, United States alignment with one side in a civil war.

The American failure to destroy quickly the Vietnamese revolution has now begun to erode the impressive successes the United States has had in defining an immensely profitable relationship to most Third World economies. But ultimately, as many in Washington well realize, the major cost of Vietnam will not be its impact on gold and trade balances, but the weakening of United States resolve and ability to interfere in the domestic affairs of nations everywhere, making both increasingly possible and plausible to others the revolutionary path, one that even the greatest intervention in history by the strong against the seemingly weak could not bar. To the oppressed peasants in Brazil or Peru the outcome in Vietnam will not influence their ultimate actions, but where leadership cadres may play a vital role the many lessons of Vietnam will not be lost. Immediately, however, the war in Vietnam has accelerated certain latent weaknesses that the United States, sooner or later, would have had to face in its dealings with European capitalism.

In this book I concentrate mainly on the economic strength of the United States in relationship to the Third World because it is here, for reasons which I make clear, that the United States has intervened continuously in numerous, diverse ways in regions where abstract questions of internal political forms are irrelevant to American security, save as they threaten United States economic interests. The precise nature, extent, and importance of those interests I will specify in an effort to give some larger content and meaning to American global interventionism. However, as I also suggest in Chapter Three, despite America's great power over the Third World economies, for over a decade its competition with Europe for domination in many key aspects of the world economy has consistently undermined its supremacy. Combined with the seemingly endless cost of the Vietnam war, this competition has seriously, and perhaps fatally, sapped whatever decisive advantages the United States holds in the total world economy. The result is reflected in what is superficially called the "gold" or "dollar" crisis. In fact what is at stake is the long-term future of American economic power as it overextends itself in the hopeless, openended task of policing the world.

United States mastery over the world economy, especially in the decade after 1945, was due more to Europe's political follies and rival imperialisms from 1900 to 1945, and less to inherent American economic talent and resources than most analysts would care to admit. Insularity and caution, in effect, combined to allow the United States to avoid most of their consequences while Europe engaged in two massive, prolonged bloodlettings and orgies of destruction. After the mid-1950's, however, the Western European nations began achieving those significant economic gains in industry and export I itemize in the chapter on the world economy, and the United States committed itself to costly and increasingly bloody policies that further benefited European power in global trade. The so-called gold and dollar crisis is the combination of all these postwar factors leading to a new distribution of world economic power in which Europe will, at this rate, increasingly define the rules of the game. The acrimonious GATT tariff and trade negotiations expressed this competition between the United States and Europe for some years. Today the controversy is over the value of a dollar which makes possible United States military bases everywhere, a relatively cheaper Vietnam war, and greater American investment in Europe and the world than the other capitalist nations now care to see. The devaluation of the dollar will make increasingly expensive and implausible Washington's application of all these financial and military policies at one and the same time, further strengthening Europe's advantage in the world economy.

The gold crisis, the deeper and more fundamental shifts in power beneath it, and the Vietnam debacle have begun to reveal not only the limits of United States power in the world but also the structure, content, and purposes of American policy. A coherent social theory must take into account both the sources and objectives of American diplomacy and also its capacity to achieve its goals. Any assessment of the future of American society which fails to relate power and class, domestic and foreign policy, does not do justice to the integrated nature of the existing social system, the manner in which the Cold War gave a temporary respite to the system's internal economic problems of poverty, automation, and the like, and how the failure of America's global strategy will open up new options and tensions at home. No one can predict the scope, intensity, and timing of this constriction of American might, but it is sufficient that the very existence of these weaknesses creates new possibilities for social change at home, and in any event reveals the inexorable lesson of modern history: that no nation can guide the destinies of the entire world.

Vietnam is both the most dramatic reflection and a cause of the United States' present malaise. It sharpens the character and reveals the potential danger and inhumanity of American globalism as no other event has in our lifetime. It is a futile effort to contain the irrepressible belief that men can control their own fates and transform their own societies, a notion that is utterly incompatible with an integrated world system ordered to benefit the United States' material welfare. Vietnam exposes the inability of Washington to restrain the overflowing national revolutionary movements. In the context of what the United States has to lose should its immense undertaking fail, Vietnam grotesquely highlights, as does no other event, the interests and objectives of those men of power who today direct this nation's foreign policy. This book of essays is an effort to describe the critical aspects of the institutional and historical setting in which America has directed its power in the past decade or so, an attempt to define more sharply the notion of causes in American diplomacy and, above all, to reintroduce the concepts of interest and power into our understanding of American society at home and its role abroad.

THE ROOTS OF

AMERICAN FOREIGN POLICY

THE MEN OF POWER

TO COMPREHEND the nature and function of power in America is to uncover a critical analytic tool for assessing the character of the American historical experience and the role of the United States in the modern world. The failure of most of an entire generation of American intellectuals and scholars to make the phenomenon of power a central concern has permitted a fog of obscuritanism and irrelevance to descend upon the study of American life in the twentieth century.

Stated simply, the question is: What are the political and economic dimensions of power in American society, how does power function, and who benefits from it? The correlations of these structural aspects of power are either curious or critical, incidental, and perhaps colorful, or of decisive importance. The structure of power may be described empirically, but power may also reflect a more elusive configuration of social attitudes and forces that makes it possible for one class to prevail in American history—or it may involve aspects of both the tangible and the intangible.

For the most part, the handful of students of American power have concentrated on the investigation of the social status and origins of men of power, an exercise that has meaning only if one can show distinctive political behavior on the part of men of power with lower social status. Indeed, one must assess the psychology of decision-makers, the genesis of their power, and the source of their conduct in the context of the structure and function of American power at home and in the world, a critical evaluation that permits one to determine whether a "military-industrial complex," a unique bureaucratic mentality, or something more substantial is the root of American policy nationally and internationally. It forces us to determine whether, for example, the presence of a Harriman-family lawyer in one key post is, in itself, crucial to understanding the goals and motives of his behavior and American policies, or whether powerful men freely use one decision-making mechanism or another in a situation in which the results are largely the same because more fundamental interests and goals define the range of action and objectives of all decision-makers. The permanence and continuity in American national and international policy for the better part of this century, scaled to the existence and possibilities of growing national strength, suggests that the study of power in America must also define the nature and function of American interests at the same time.

If, in the last analysis, the structure of power can only be understood in the context in which it functions and the goals American power seeks to attain, the fact that the magnitude of such a vast description requires a full history of twentieth century America should not deter social analysts from highlighting the larger contours of the growth of modern American bureaucracies, if only to make the crucial point that these bureaucratic structures are less the source of power than the means by which others direct power in America for predetermined purposes. That society is one in which bureaucrats do not represent their own tangible interests, save if they wear other and more important hats, but those of what one must tentatively call that of the "power system," and when their own aspirations become dysfunctional leaders remove them on behalf of more pliable men. For behind the bureaucrats exist levels of economic and political power, whether latent or exercised, the objectives and maintenance of which no one can abandon without far-reaching, indeed revolutionary, alterations in policy and the very nature of American society itself. It is this ultimate power that defines the limits of bureaucratic conduct and the functions of the state.

Politicians create bureaucracies for specific purposes, and that these structures develop their own administrative codes and techniques, or complex mystifying rationales, is less consequential than their objective and functions. Congress created such bureaucratic power in the United States first during the era 1887–1917 as a result of class-oriented elements seeking to rationalize via political systems the unpredictable elements of economic life in a modern technology. To study *how* rather than *why* political power operates in a class society, a formalism that Max Weber contributed to conservative descriptive social analysis, is to avoid the central issue of the class nature and function of the modern state. After the turn of the century the political parties cultivated bureaucracy purely as an instrumentality serving and reflecting class interests—bureaucracy with no independent power base and nowhere to find one within the American power structure. Given the decisive role of the businessmen in the creation of modern American bureaucracy and the "positive state," it should be neither surprising nor impractical that they staff the higher levels of the bureaucratic mechanisms of American power with men from business.

Policy, in brief, preceded bureaucratic rationalism, with Congress serving as a lobby for, and objective of, various business interests. Given the consensual nature of social and political priorities in America, and the essentially repressive manner in which the authorities handle nonconformity to consensus when it becomes a potential threat, political power in American society is an aspect of economic power—economic power often sharply in conflict by region or size or interest, but always operative within certain larger assumptions about the purposes of victory for one side or the other. Often this disunity among competing economic interests is so great as to mean mutual neutralization and ineffectuality, and frequently the divergent factions couch their goals in rhetorical terms— "anti-monopoly" being the most overworked—which has made "liberal" phraseology the useful ideology of corporate capitalism.

This diversity and conflict within the ranks of business and politicians, usually described as a pluralist manifestation, has attracted more attention than it deserves and leads to amoebic descriptions of the phenomenon of interbusiness rivalry in a manner that obscures the much more significant dimensions of common functions and objectives. The critical question for the study of what passes as conflict in American society must be: What are the major positions, and who wins and why? The motives of the losers in the game of politics, or of those who created pressures others redirected for their own ends, is less critical than the actual distribution of power in society. It is in this context of the nature of power and its function that the scholar should study bureaucracies, with less concern for social mobility than the concept of purpose and goals the bureaucracy serves. Only in this manner can we understand the interests and actions that are functional and irrevocable as part of the logic of American power and not the result of mishap, personalities, or chance. If powerful economic groups are geographically diffuse and often in competition for particular favors from the state, superficially appearing as interest groups rather than as a unified class, what is critical is not who wins or loses but what kind of socioeconomic framework they *all* wish to compete within, and the relationship between themselves and the rest of society in a manner that defines their vital function as a class. It is this class that controls the major policy options and the manner in which the state applies its power. That they disagree on the options is less consequential than that they circumscribe the political universe.[1]

Despite the increasingly technical character of modern political and economic policy, and the need to draw on individuals with appropriate backgrounds for the administration of policy —especially businessmen—it is the structural limits and basic economic objectives of policy that define the thrust of American power nationally and internationally. The source of leadership is important, and has been since the turn of the century, but it may not be decisive. What is ultimately of greatest significance is that whether leadership comes from Exeter-Harvard or Kansas, the results have been the same, and an outcome of the nature of power in America and the role of the United States in the world.

The Limits of Consensus

American politics in the twentieth century has been a process of change and shifting rewards within predictable boundaries and commitments that are ultimately conservative and controlled as to the limited social and economic consequences it may achieve. No decisive or shattering social and economic goals have cracked the basic structure and distribution of power in all its forms, and if some have used democratic and liberal rhetoric to explain motion within these boundaries it is less consequential than the functional material contours of the system itself. Indeed, it is the illusion of the possibility of significant change—of true freedom in society—that helps make possible its practical suppression via liberal politics and gradualism which, as historical fact, never exceed predetermined orbits and assumptions.

One must never infer that such illusions are the sole source of conservative order—as witnessed by the response of those with power during rare periods when genuine opposition shatters the mythologies. For though freedom is a posture decision-makers tolerate among the politically impotent, those in power act to make certain that all others remain ineffectual. When their own policies are subject to severe trials, or appear to be failing, they cannot afford the luxury of organized opposition and functional freedoms which can shatter their hegemony over the normal, usually passive social apathy. The history of civil liberties in the United States is testimony to the fact that when freedom moves from rhetoric to social challenge it is suppressed insofar as is necessary. Functional freedom is the ability to relate to power or forces with the potential for achieving authority, that is, the decision-making establishment or those who seek to transform or replace it. So long as intellectuals or the people exercise this right "responsibly," which is to say to endorse and serve the consensus their rulers define, abstract freedoms flourish in public pronouncements and slogans because they lead nowhere. Hence the dissenter has the freedom to become a victim in the social process and history, and a battery of sedition, espionage, criminal anarchy, or labor laws exist in readiness for the appropriate moment of social tension and the breakdown in the social and ideological consensus which exists during periods of peace and stability. The celebrants of American freedom rarely confront the concepts of order that underlie the large body of law for suppression that always exists in reserve.

A theory of consensus is indispensable for comprehending the nature of decision-making and power in American society, but a social analyst must always consider that theory from the viewpoint of its role when some socially critical and potentially dynamic groups and classes cease to endorse or sanction the consensus, because then consensus is based on discipline and becomes, for practical purposes, authoritarian on matters of measurable power. For only challenges to a political and social system and crises reveal its true character—when established power threatens to break down and formal democracy is nearly transformed into functional, true freedom.

The essential, primary fact of the American social system is that it is a capitalist society based on a grossly inequitable distribution of wealth and income that has not been altered in any essential manner in this century. Even if there has not been *decisive* class conflict within that structure, but merely conflict limited to smaller issues that were not crucial to the existing order, one can accurately describe American society as a static class structure serving class ends. A sufficiently monolithic consensus might voluntarily exist on the fundamental questions indispensable to the continuation of the existing political and economic elites, and the masses might respect or tolerate the primary interest of a ruling class in the last analysis. The prevailing conception of interests, the critical values of the society, did not have to be essentially classless, as Louis Hartz and recent theorists of consensus have argued, but merely accepted by those segments of society without an objective stake in the constituted order. This dominant class, above all else, determines the nature and objectives of power in America. And for this reason no one can regard business as just another interest group in American life, but as the keystone of power which defines the essential preconditions and functions of the larger American social order, with its security and continuity as an institution being the political order's central goal in the post-Civil War historical experience.

On the national level, reform and legislation have led to class ends and the satisfaction of class needs, and that the purposes of decision-makers in 1968 should be any different than in 1888 makes sense only if one can posit and prove a drastic alteration in the distribution of economic power.

One may base such an analysis on a functional view of American reform, on the consequences of legislation rather than the motives of all reformers, motives that are ultimately paramount among those who are to be regulated and who have power. Social theory, muckrakers, and intellectuals did not and do not influence important businessmen, who have never aspired to have reforming crusaders regulate and direct their affairs. Businessmen have always preferred that their own lawyers and direct representatives play that role in matters of the most intimate relevance to their economic fortunes, though not necessarily in lesser affairs, and it is a fact that the government has ultimately drawn most critical political decision-makers from, or into, the higher reaches of economic life. In this setting, we should see American reform primarily as a question of technical and efficiency engineering—of social rationalization—to advance the welfare and interests of specific business interests first and society generally, but always within critical ideological boundaries and assumptions. With only occasional differences on tangential points, political authorities have shared, or conformed to, the practical applications of this conservative consolidation usually called "progressivism" or "liberalism."

Yet the critical question arises as to why, in such an economic context of inequality, poverty, and many years of unemployment, there has never been a class opposition to constituted politics and power. In brief, quite apart from the efficacy of the alternatives, why has no anti-capitalist mass movement emerged, as in Western Europe, to create that essential political option which is the indispensable precondition for true pluralism and freedom in America? For the United States is a class society, with measurable oppression, but also without decisive class conflict as of this time. It is also a society serving class ends with the consensual support or apathetic toleration of the dispossessed classes. This consensus, which serves the interest of a single class rather than all of society, exists in an altogether different situation than what theorists of consensus have described, but the social and historic outcome is the same.

The phenomenon of consensus and its causes are simply too complex to describe in light of existing evidence. But it is necessary to pose certain critical questions in order to comprehend whether consent alone is important in explaining the nature and durability of American power and the decision-making structure. What happens when the consensus is shattered and ceases to receive traditional adherence or toleration? Does the fact that all of society may at times share an ideology legitimate it? Or is it more consequential that the economically critical and powerful class endorses the ideology that serves it best—a fact that makes the ideology operate during those rare periods when consensus breaks down? And can core commitments of the public be evaluated by any measurable techniques that permit valid social generalization?

If the history of Left politics in the United States is co-option for some, it is also repression for many others: grandfather clauses, poll taxes, and other means for applying the stick when the carrot was insufficient or deemed inappropriate. The history of the militant labor movement, black struggles, southern populism, socialism, and even the current anti-war and civil rights movements all bear testimony to the fact that when politics and social movements do not legitimize the existing order consensus becomes mandatory conformity and suppression. Authority and power exist quite beyond general social sanctions and rest on specific interests and the ability to impose restraints, and the ruling class has never permitted decision-makers in the governmental apparatus who do not advance and conform to the interests of the state—for psychological reasons or whatever—to introduce dysfunctional elements or policies into governmental affairs. This enforced consensus from above and social cohesion due to the relatively rare exercise of ever latent authority and repression has been the truly revealing aspect of the nature and purpose of American power and capitalist interests. Yet whether voluntaristic or otherwise, these shared values make the origins of decision-makers, or the identity of their special governmental agencies, less consequential than the binding and permanent commitments of ruling groups and their social and economic system.

For this reason, mass consent in a society based on a relatively small elite predominance is less significant, and the operative causal agents in society are the interests and goals of men of power—and their will and ability to retain their mastery—rather than masses who also endorse those objectives. It is the commitments of those able to implement their beliefs and goals, rather than of the powerless, that creates racism in the employment practices of corporations; and it is elite authoritarianism, which remains constant in the historical process, rather than working class biases—which vary with circumstances and interest and often disappear functionally—that leads to authoritarian institutions.

Yet even if the social and power weight of specific opinion and class interests, as opposed to its existence among all sectors of society, is primary, it is still vital to comprehend the elusive character of what is now called "public opinion" or "consensus." What is more significant than opinion is the ultimate implications of apathy and ignorance of elite sanctioned policies, a condition that reveals the limits of the integrative possibilities of elite-controlled "mass culture" from above. For the most part, in matters of foreign affairs, workers are no more or less belligerent or pacifistic than executives and professionals—when they are forced to register an opinion. The theory of public attitudes as the fount of the decision-making process reinforces a democratic theory of legitimacy, which, for reasons of sentimental tradition at home and ideological warfare abroad, is a useful social myth. But the close and serious student of modern American foreign relations will rarely, if ever, find an instance of an important decision made with any reference to the alleged general public desires or opinions. What is more significant is the fact of ignorance and lack of interest among the vast majority of the population during a period of crisis as to the nature of essential issues and facts, a condition that neutralizes their role in the decision-making process even more and cultivates an elitist contempt for the inchoate role of "the people" as nothing more than the instrument or objective, rather than the source, of policy.[2] The persistent fluctuations in such mass attitudes alone assure that for practical guidance the decision-makers must refer to their own tangible and constant values and priorities. Yet what no one has ever shown is the extent to which this mass apathy reflects the manipulative and moronizing impact of modern communications, or a superior intelligence based on the individual's awareness that he has no power or influence after all, and that he has a very different identity and interest in the social process than the managers and rulers of society.

The Versatile Rulers

If the manipulated values and consensual ideology coincide with the objective and material interests of the decision-makers, the fact is important but not necessarily the sole causal factor of their conduct, for even where personal interests do not exist the policies are the same. The function of bureaucracy is to serve constituted power, not itself. While it often can be relevant that an individual in government is directly connected with a business interest, even one in a field deeply concerned with the topic over which he has jurisdiction, we can determine the ultimate significance of this connection only if more disinterested men adopt different policies. Historically, by and large, they have not. In our own era the reasons for this continuity in policy and action are critical, and they reveal the institutional and interest basis of American power in the world, a power that transcends factions and men.

American diplomacy has traditionally been the prerogative of the rich and well placed. Even if they had a lifetime career in government, the intrinsic nature of the structure until 1924 required professional diplomats to be men of independent means, and that tradition persisted until today in various forms. In 1924 the Diplomatic Corps, which paid salaries so low that only the sons of the well-to-do and rich could advance very far in it, was merged with the Consular Corps into the Foreign Service to establish a merit system. In 1924, 63 percent of the diplomatic officers were Harvard-Princeton-Yale graduates, as opposed to 27 percent of the ambassadors for the years 1948, 1958, and 1963. Of the 1,032 key federal executive appointees between March 4, 1933, and April 30, 1965, 19 percent had attended these three elite schools, ranging from 16 percent under Roosevelt to 25 percent during the Johnson Administration. Somewhat lower on the scale of rank, in 1959 the three universities produced 14 percent of all Foreign Service executives, while nearly two-thirds of those in the Service were the sons of business executives and owners or professionals. At the level of all civilian federal executives above GS-18 ranking, or the very highest group, 58 percent were the sons of this upper income and status occupational category.[3]

Sociologists such as C. Wright Mills, and often journalists as well, have made too much of these social origins, for while interesting and important there is no proof such connections are decisive. Twenty-six percent of the highest federal executives come from working class and farmer origins, and an increasingly larger percentage from the non-Ivy League schools, and there is no evidence whatsoever to prove that social and educational origins determine policies of state. That elite origins and connections accelerated personal advancement is now sufficiently self-evident not to warrant excessive attention, much less to make these standards the key criterion for explaining the sources and purposes of American power. In brief, the basic objectives, function, and exercise of American power, and not simply its formal structure and identity, are paramount in defining its final social role and significance. Without denigrating the important contribution of Mills, which was brilliant but inconsistent, such an approach fails to come to grips with the dynamics of American power in its historical setting.

A class structure and predatory rule can exist within the context of high social mobility and democratic criteria for rulership, perhaps all the better so because it co-opts the elites and experts of the potential opposition and totally integrates talent into the existing society. The major value in essentially static structural studies of key decision-makers is to illustrate the larger power context in which administrators made decisions, but not to root the nature of those decisions in the backgrounds or individual personalities of an elite. In brief, correlation may not be causation in the power structure, and should high status, rich men ever seek to make decisions dysfunctional to the more permanent interests of dominant power interests, even more powerful leaders would immediately purge them from decision-making roles. The point is that while such men are unlikely to make socially dysfunctional decisions so is anyone else who rises to the top of a structure with predetermined rules and functions. To measure power that is latent as well as active, it is often easier to study the decision-makers themselves. The other approach, and by far the more difficult, is to define objective and impersonal interests and roles for the larger classes and sectors of American society, their relationship to each other and to the world, and the manner in which they have exercised their relative power.

The analyst must utilize both approaches, and should consider everything useful, including the investigation of status, celebrities, core elites, military elites—the important and trivial, as Mills discovered—and he should discount the trivial and establish the correlations in the hope of revealing causes. If Mills made it clear that there were levels of power among those who shared it, and an inner power core that transcended local society and celebrities, he slighted the economic basis of American politics and exaggerated the causal and independent importance of the military.[4] To him, the social and educational origins of the elite were too critical, thereby excluding the possibility of a power elite "democratized" within its own ranks or selection process but still in the traditional dominant relationship to the remainder of society. Offhand, I assume that in this process it is worth striking a final balance and integration and rejecting certain factors. Social origins and education, and the possibility of the existence of an Establishment based on common heritage and interests, are of lesser concern than the currently operative ties of decision-makers, for the father's words or the impressions of old school days wear off, and the responsibilities of men are measurable in the present rather than in the past.

★

A more select group reveals far more than a collection as large as W. Lloyd Warner's 12,929 federal executives, and on this assumption I investigated the career cycles and origins of the key American foreign policy decision-makers from 1944 through 1960, excluding the Presidents. My major premise was that even if I could show that such men neither began nor ended in business, there were still many other and more valid ways of gauging the nature of foreign policy. We examined the State, Defense or War, Treasury and Commerce Departments, plus certain relevant executive level agencies indicated in the "Note on Methods" on page 140, and considered only those with the highest ranks.[5] The study included 234 individuals with all their positions in government during 1944–60, comprising the lesser posts if an individual attained the highest executive level. As a total, these key leaders held 678 posts and nearly all of them were high level and policy-making in nature.

The net result of this study, however imperfect, revealed that foreign policy decision-makers are in reality a highly mobile sector of the American corporate structure, a group of men who frequently assume and define high level policy tasks in government, rather than routinely administer it, and then return to business. Their firms and connections are large enough to afford them the time to straighten out or formulate government policy while maintaining their vital ties with giant corporate law, banking, or industry. The conclusion is that a small number of men fill the large majority of key foreign policy posts. Their many diverse posts make this group a kind of committee government entrusted to handle numerous and varied national security and international functions at the policy level. Even if not initially connected with the corporate sector, career government officials relate in some tangible manner with the private worlds predominantly of big law, big finance, and big business.

Of the 234 officials examined, 35.8 percent, or eighty-four individuals, held 63.4 percent of the posts (Table I). Thirty men from law, banking, and investment firms accounted for 22 percent of all the posts which we studied, and another fifty-seven from this background held an additional 14.1 percent—or a total of 36.1 percent of the key posts. Certain key firms predominated among this group: members of Sullivan &

TABLE I

OCCUPATIONAL ORIGIN OF INDIVIDUALS WITH FOUR OR MORE POSTS IN GOVERNMENT AND THOSE WITH LESS THAN FOUR POSTS, 1944–60

Occupational Origin	Individuals with Four or More Posts				Individuals with Less Than Four Posts			
	No. of Individuals	% of All Individuals	No. of Posts Held	% of All Posts Studied	No. of Individuals	% of All Individuals	No. of Posts Held	% of All Posts Studied
Law Firms	12	5.1	55	8.1	33	14.1	72	10.6
Banking and Investment Firms	18	7.7	94	13.9	24	10.3	24	3.5
Industrial Corporations	8	3.4	39	5.8	31	13.2	49	7.2
Public Utilities and Transportation Companies	0	.0	0	.0	4	1.7	4	.6
Miscellaneous Business and Commercial Firms	7	3.0	32	4.7	17	7.3	35	5.2
Nonprofit Corporations, Public Service, Universities, etc.	7	3.0	37	5.5	7	3.0	12	1.8
Career Government Officials—No Subsequent Nongovernment Post	15	6.4	85	12.5	11	4.7	19	2.8
Career Government Officials—Subsequent Nongovernment Post	8	3.4	38	5.6	12	5.1	13	1.9
Career Government Officials—Subsequent Nongovernment Post and Return to Government Post	8	3.4	45	6.6	6	2.6	15	2.2
Unidentified	1	.4	5	.7	5	2.1	5	.7
TOTALS	84	35.8	430	63.4	150	64.1	248	36.5

Cromwell, or Carter, Ledyard & Milburn, and Coudert Brothers, in that order among law firms, held twenty-nine posts, with other giant corporate-oriented law firms accounting for most of the remainder. Dillon, Read & Co., with four men, and the Detroit Bank, with only Joseph M. Dodge, accounted for eighteen and ten posts, respectively, and two men from Brown Brothers, Harriman held twelve posts—or forty posts for three firms. It was in the nature of their diverse functions as lawyers and financiers for many corporate industrial and investment firms, as Mills correctly perceived, that these men preeminently represented the less parochial interests of all giant corporations, and were best able to wear many hats and play numerous roles, frequently and interchangeably as each corporate or government problem—or both—required. Nothing reveals this dual function more convincingly than their career cycles. Despite the fact that Sullivan & Cromwell and Dillon, Read men tended to go into the State Department, or lawyers from Cahill, Gordon, Zachry & Riendel to the Navy Department, general patterns of distribution by economic interests—save for bankers in the governmental banking structure—are not discernible. And with one possible exception, all the men from banking, investment, and law who held four or more posts were connected with the very largest and most powerful firms in these fields.

In the aggregate, men who came from big business, investment, and law held 59.6 percent of the posts, with only forty-five of them filling 32.4 percent of all posts[6] (Tables I and II). The very top foreign policy decision-makers were therefore intimately connected with dominant business circles and their law firms. And whether exercised or not, scarcely concealed levels of economic power exist beneath or behind the government, and indeed high mobility in various key posts reinforces such interlockings. This continuous reality has not altered with successive administrations, as the state has called upon

TABLE II

NUMBER OF KEY POSITIONS IN GOVERNMENT, 1944–60, HELD BY

Nongovernment and Career Government Category	No. of Individuals	% of Individuals	State Dept.	Defense Dept.	War Dept.	Treasury Dept.	Commerce Dept.
[1] Key Law Firms	45	19.2	16	12	12	7	1
[2] Banking and Investment Firms	42	17.9	19	7	3	8	7
[3] Industrial Corporations	39	16.7	9	5	1	2	12
[4] Public Utilities and Transportation Corporations	4	1.7					
[5] Miscellaneous Business and Commercial Corporations	24	10.3	8	5		3	1
TOTAL: 1–5	154	65.8	52	29	16	20	21
[6] Nonprofit, Public Service, and Universities	14	6.0	4		1	1	1
TOTAL: 1–6	168	71.8	56	29	17	21	22
[7] Career Officials—No Subsequent Nongovernment Position	26	11.1	26	1	1	4	2
[8] Career Officials—Subsequent Nongovernment Position	20	8.5	7	4	1	2	2
[9] Career Officials—Subsequent Nongovernment Position and Return to Government	14	6.0	12	5	1	1	1
TOTAL: 7–9	60	25.6	45	10	3	7	5
UNIDENTIFIED	6	2.6	1			1	
COMBINED TOTAL	234	99.9	102	39	20	29	27

INDIVIDUALS DESIGNATED BY NONGOVERNMENT CAREER ORIGIN AND BY A GOVERNMENT CAREER ORIGIN

Navy Dept.	Army Dept.	Air Force Dept.	White House Staff	International Bank for Reconstruction and Development	Export-Import Bank	E.C.A.—M.S.A.—I.C.A.	Budget Bureau	C.I.A.	Japan and German Military Governments	Miscellaneous Government Departments	No. of Positions	% of Positions
15	8	8	2	1		4	2	5	3	31	127	18.7
8	4	1	4	7	4	8	3	1	4	30	118	17.4
1	4	9	3	1		9		1		31	88	13.0
1	1		1			1					4	.6
8	2	2	5			12	6			15	67	9.9
33	**18**	**21**	**14**	**9**	**5**	**33**	**12**	**7**	**7**	**107**	**404**	**59.6**
	2	1	3			10	4	3	3	16	49	7.2
33	**20**	**22**	**17**	**9**	**5**	**43**	**16**	**10**	**10**	**123**	**453**	**66.8**
	2			3	7	10	4	1		43	104	15.5
3	2	2	5			4	4	1	4	10	51	7.5
4	1		2		1	9	2	1	1	19	60	8.8
7	5	2	2	8	8	23	10	3	5	72	215	31.8
			2	1	2	1	1			1	10	1.5
40	25	24	21	18	15	67	27	13	15	196	678	100.1

Fair Dealers and modern Republicans alike to serve as experts in running a going operation which they are asked to administer efficiently within certain common definitions of its objectives. Whether Democrats, such as James Forrestal of Dillon, Read, or Republicans, such as John Foster Dulles of Sullivan & Cromwell, the continuous contact and advice they have received from their colleagues in the world of finance, law, and business have always colored their focus. The operative assumption of such men, as Forrestal once put it, is that "What I have been trying to preach down here is that in this whole world picture the Government alone can't do the job; it's got to work through business. . . . that means that we'll need to, for specific jobs, be able to tap certain people. . . ."[7] It is this process of "tapping" for high level policy tasks that has accounted for high mobility and the concentration of posts in few hands.

Perhaps of even greater interest is the special nature of the government career officials and their relationship to business during their extended professional lives. These sixty men, 25.6 percent of the total, held 31.7 percent of the posts considered, in part because, being full-timers, they were available for a greater number of tasks. But for many of these men government became a stepping stone toward business careers, and we can only speculate on how this possible aspiration influenced their functional policies on economic and other questions while they were in government. "The lure of industry was such that I couldn't pass it up," a former career officer and head of the C.I.A. for fourteen months, Admiral William F. Raborn, Jr., confessed in discussing why he had taken his government post in the first place. "I went there with the thought I could go when I wanted to."[8] Over half these men, perhaps enticed in the same manner, later took up nongovernmental posts, though a significant fraction returned to government for special tasks. Conversely, however, any government employee thwarting the interests of American businesses, as expressed in foreign and national security affairs, risks losing possible future posts, even if he goes to foundations or university administrations. Most of these new private positions were in law firms and industry. But certain of those key career officials who never left for business or new careers the State Department had selected under its pre-1924 or conventional rules, where independent wealth and social connections were always helpful. The fact that John M. Cabot, Assistant Secretary of State and a Boston Cabot, also held the largest number of posts among the twenty-six full-time career officials we examined is not inconsequential. It is within this career group that the conventional elite social background predominates.

For the most part, the technical and policy nature of foreign policy and military security issues has necessitated the selection of men with requisite business backgrounds. The choice of William L. Clayton, rags-to-riches head of the largest world cotton export firm, to deal with United States foreign economic policy between 1944–47 was rational and both a cause and reflection of policy.[9] What is most instructive was that Woodrow Wilson and Cordell Hull, President and Secretary of State (1933–44), a professor and small town politician, formulated the essential foreign economic policy, and it is here that we must see the larger ideological and consensual definition of foreign policy as ultimately transcending the decision-maker recruitment process.

Business as the Fount

The organizational rungs of governmental power take many other businessmen into the lower hierarchies of administration in much the same manner as their seniors function at the very highest levels. These lower tiers of operation are too extensive to measure in their entirety here, but it is sufficient to point to several readily documented expressions. Such lines of contact are perfectly logical, given the objectives of American policy abroad, and given the fact that Washington generally assigns the management of the Government's relationship to various problems to the businessmen or their representatives with business connections or backgrounds in the various areas. And it is both convenient and more than logical that key federal executives recruit former associates for critical problem-solving posts for which they have responsibility. There is no conflict of interest because the welfare of government and business is, in the largest sense, identical.

This will mean that key law firm executives with major corporate connections will draw on former clients, whom they may again soon represent at the termination of their governmental service; it will simplify the task of the business representatives in Washington—about two-thirds of the top two hundred manufacturing firms maintain them on a full-time basis—who may wish assistance with marketing, legislative, or legal matters. The Government will invariably choose advisers to international raw materials and commodity meetings from the consuming industries, and will select key government executives concerned with specific issues—such as oil—from the interested industry. The existence of businessmen and their lawyers in government, in short, gives the lobbyists and those not in government something to do—successfully—insofar as it is to their interest. These men interact in different roles and at various times, for today's assistant secretary may be tomorrow's senior partner or corporate president. However much such men may have competing specific economic objectives, conflicts that may indeed at times neutralize their mutual goals, what is essentially common among such elites, whether or not they are cooperative, makes them a class with joint functions and assumptions and larger economic objectives that carry with it the power to rule. This is not to say such well placed officials with industry backgrounds are the only source of government policy, but that they exist and, more important, given the larger aims of government it is entirely rational to select personnel in this fashion. From this viewpoint the nature of the bureaucracy is essentially an outcome rather than a cause of policy.

Examples of interlocking government-business leadership are numerous even below the highest decision-making echelons. In the Department of the Interior, to cite one instance, the large majority of key personnel in the Office of Oil and Gas or the Petroleum Administration for Defense in the decade after 1946 came from the industry, often just on loan for fixed periods of time. These bodies, which are largely a continuation of wartime boards, have permitted the regulation of the petroleum industry via governmental agencies, free from the threat of antitrust prosecution and for the welfare of the industry. Pleased with the arrangement, the industry has supplied many of the key administrators and consultants the government needs on a no-compensation basis.[10]

No less typical is the Business and Defense Services Administration of the Department of Commerce (BDSA), created in the fall of 1953. Composed of 184 industry groups during the period 1953–55, the BDSA committees dealt with a vast number of goods and the problems of their industry, recommending action to the government that was the basis of profitable action and regulation of various economic sectors. These ranged from the division of government purchases among industry members to the review of proposed Export-Import Bank and World Bank loans for the construction of competing industries abroad. In effect, BDSA committees have served themselves via the government in a classic fashion, the precedents for which range back to the early nineteenth century.[11] In this regard they are no different in genesis and function from the federal regulatory movement initiated in 1887.

★

At every level of the administration of the American state, domestically and internationally, business serves as the fount of critical assumptions or goals and strategically placed personnel. But that this leadership in foreign and military affairs, as integrated in the unified hands of men who are both political and economic leaders, comes from the most powerful class interests is a reflection as well as the cause of the nature and objectives of American power at home and abroad. It is the expression of the universality of the ideology *and* the interests and material power of the physical resources of the ruling class of American capitalism, the latter being sufficient should consensus break down. The pervasiveness of this ideological power in American society and its measurable influence on mass culture, public values, and political opinions is the most visible reality of modern American life to the contemporary social analyst. It means that one can only assess the other institutional structures, the military in particular, in relation to the predominance of the economic ruling class which is the final arbiter and beneficiary of the existing structure of American society and politics at home and of United States power in the world.

THE AMERICAN
MILITARY AND CIVIL AUTHORITY

IN THE UNITED STATES the civilians, the self-styled "liberals" and "democrats," finally direct the application of American power in all its forms throughout the world. Despite the dramatic and sinister overtones in the phrase "military-industrial complex," or C. Wright Mills' vision of "the military ascendancy," the fact is that the nature of global conflict and the means of violence are so thoroughly political and economic in their essential character, so completely intricate technologically, that it is probably more correct to argue the case for the declining importance of the military in the decision-making structure. For military power is the instrument American political leaders utilize to advance their enormous and ever-growing objectives, and that they require a vast Military Establishment is the logical, necessary effect rather than the cause of the basic objectives and momentum of American foreign policy since 1943. Civilians formulated that policy, in the context of the critical postwar period, when the Military Establishment was docile and relatively starved. Belligerence requires generals and arms as tools for the advancement of permanent objectives.

The critics of America's policies in the world have focused their attacks on the visibility of the military, as if its "liberalization" would transform the reality of America's global role. The notion of an independent military dynamic and ethic occludes the real interests and purposes of American foreign policy, which is not to fight wars but to gain vital strategic and economic objectives that materially enlarge American power everywhere. That the military is a neutral instrumentality of civilian policy is inherent in the fact that increasingly the major object of strategic military policy is how to avoid using suicidal nuclear armaments while successfully advancing American economic and political goals. These ends are active, the struggle for them the potential cause of nuclear conflict that could destroy the world; only the most extreme imperatives ever led the civilians to consider this risk and option. If a distinctive military ethic, a regenerative theory of bloodletting and heroism, has ever existed, it has not caused a war in which civilian men of power did not first conceive of some more rational, material goals. This is no less true of the Cold War than of the Spanish-American War, when Washington used an essentially civilian-inspired theoretical school of heroism, which Theodore Roosevelt, Henry and Brooks Adams, and their friends led, as an ideological frosting for advancing American colonialism and global economic power.

Modern warfare is utilitarian to the furtherance of present American objectives, but only so long as it is combat between unequals and excludes great nuclear powers. This means, in brief, that in a world of revolutionary nationalist movements there are many small wars that the United States may choose to fight without confronting the U.S.S.R. or China, and that the strategic and most expensive section of the American Military Establishment will remain restrained and passive, as it has in a disciplined fashion in the past. What is left, from the numerous alternatives to anti-peasant, anti-revolutionary warfare with tiny powers, is a choice of political options for relating to the Third World, policies that civilian political leaders and their experts always determine and often call upon the military to implement. In some instances, such as Iran, Indonesia, Greece, and Cuba, the half-political, quasi-military C.I.A. has offered policy-makers more graceful-appearing means for attaining goals while skirting the more cumbersome and overt regular military. Indeed, the very existence of the C.I.A., completely removed from the military services, has increasingly strengthened the total control of the civilians over physical power and military intelligence. If the constantly changing technological escalation of the arms race has given the Military Establishment a dynamic and ever-growing appearance, we must never forget the fact that this is an effect rather than a cause of political policy, an appearance and instrumentality rather than the full nature of reality. If this were not the case, and the American military were all that the naïve element of the Left has blandly claimed, it would have destroyed the world some years ago.

So long as specialists in violence apply it only where and when higher authorities tell them to, a "garrison state" involving the disciplining of society and the politically-based unification of major economic and social institutions will be a rather different type of system than Harold D. Lasswell outlined nearly three decades ago.[1] Indeed, a coercive elite quite willing to undermine democracy at home as well as abroad will rule the society, even in the name of "liberalism," and it will permit global necessities to define its priorities internally, but contrary to Lasswell and Mills, the elite will not base its supremacy only on skill and efficiency—the qualifications of able bureaucrats—but also on the control or servicing of the economic, business sector of power. This dual relationship—one which uses the political structure to advance the domestic and global economic interests of American capitalists—has characterized Washington leaders for the better part of this century.

The fascination with the alleged expertise of the military, as if control of technique is equivalent to real power and implies a political conflict with existing authority, was the major defect in Mills' work no less than Lasswell's. Quite apart from the fact that the labyrinthine technological and political nature of modern warfare makes the professional soldier increasingly dependent on scientists and diplomats, Mills assumed that since the military sector generated vast economic demand, it somehow gave generals and admirals equal power, or near parity, with big business in the permanent war economy, merging their identities and interests in a distinctive, new fashion.[2] Yet how and what the government orders to attain its military goals is a much more complex process than he acknowledged, and that this created a war economy or sector should not obscure the fact that how and where—and how much—money was spent is always a decision of civilian political men as well as interested economic groups. My aim in this essay is to show that the military has always been the instrument, the effect rather than the cause of this policy. That the military intermingled with business and political leaders, and indeed shared a common social origin and outlook, is less consequential than the actual power of the various designers of American policy in the world. Quite apart from the alleged existence of what Mills called "military capitalism," the major issue is: Does this relationship serve the real interests of the military, the capitalists, or both?

Business Definition of the Military Structure

Business is both a fount and magnet for the Military Establishment. The "military-industrial complex" that exists in the United States is a lopsided phenomenon in which only businessmen maintain their full identity, interests, and commitments to their institution, while the military conforms to the needs of economic interests. Business careers are now part of the aspirations of thousands of military officers, while key businessmen and their lawyers continuously pass in and out of major bureaucratic posts in the Defense Department and national security agencies, usually remaining long enough to determine key policies and then return to business. The arms race, based on continuous technological innovations, originates as often with greedy arms firms as with generals—officers who are the instruments of the arms producers insofar as the military's strategic doctrines give the Services need for appropriate hardware. Perhaps most important, at no time has the military fully controlled or defined the budget and the vital strategic assumptions that have guided its size and allocation, for in this regard their internal bickering over limited resources has greatly diminished their ability to dictate to the civilians.

Historically, the military has always depended on business to a great extent. The Government left the mobilization of industry for military purposes during the First World War primarily in the hands of businessmen, and the interwar mobilization plans followed the wartime precedents. Corporate executives and business school social scientists dominated and lectured to the Army Industrial College for the decade and one-half after its founding in 1924. When the Roosevelt Administration finally drew up and implemented mobilization plans for the Second World War, businessmen played the vital role in its critical economic aspects, and at no time during the war did any military leader attempt to utilize the vast procurement power to foster a distinctive ideology or collective policy in the postwar period.[3]

One can hardly exaggerate the importance of the specific arms producers and industries in guiding the action of their respective, allied Services, both from the viewpoint of their making available new technical means for advancing Service strategies and eventually incorporating key military men into the military-based economy. Until about 1960, when missiles became the overlapping jurisdiction of all three major Services and traditional lines broke down somewhat, the industries supplying various modes of warfare—on the land, strategic airpower, and naval—all vied with each other for the largest possible slice of the limited military budgets. "The aircraft industry," Senator Barry Goldwater once remarked, "has probably done more to promote the Air Force than the Air Force has done itself." ". . . What appears to be intense interservice rivalry," General James M. Gavin has observed, ". . . in most cases . . . is fundamentally industrial rivalry."[4] In its ultimate and always prevalent form, such business competition determines precisely which weapons systems—which often perform essentially identical functions—the government will purchase. Indeed, in the case of the B-36 bomber and TFX plane, the existence of a firm with problems and traditional Service connections may be the primary reason for the procurement of a weapons system in the first place, even at a greater cost than is necessary. In this process of competition, the officers of various Services may line up with different companies, often merely as fronts.

To survive, weapons producers, and particularly aerospace firms, must constantly devise new weapons and systems to supersede those they have already built. In 1958–59, for example, the Navy received 486 unsolicited antisubmarine-warfare proposals from the industry, and agreed to fund 155 of them. Private risk capital first developed many of the major military aircraft, even though the Services did not see their immediate relevance, only because the corporations needed the final production contracts to operate their plants and make money. In the case of the semi-official Service associations that campaign for greater expenditures for their respective branches —the Navy League, Air Force Association, and Association of the United States Army—the financing of these lobbying activities comes from corporate dues and advertising in their journals.[5]

The ultimate discipline in making key officers subservient to the major arms firms is the hiring of retired officers, about two-thirds of whom left the military voluntarily to take up their new posts. Their ability to make favorable contacts for new careers while in the Services depends, in the last analysis, on avoiding conflicts with arms firms that can close off these lucrative posts. In 1959, the 72 largest arms suppliers alone employed 1,426 retired officers, 251 of them being of flag or general rank. Many of these former officers have special skills and background in procurement, modern weaponry, or the more technologically exotic aspects of warfare, and often meet their future employers in tax-deductible luxury. In effect, corporations are asking them to sell arms to their former military associates. "Every time I go to the Pentagon to obtain a contract for one of my constituents," one congressman complained in 1960, "I run into hundreds of retired officers."[6] Today congressmen and military officers both work for various, if competing, corporations.

The Military Ethic

Radical social scientists such as Mills, and conservatives such as Samuel P. Huntington, nurtured the myth that a distinctive military ethic exists, common only to men in uniform. But the concept of aristocracy and discipline allegedly defining the military system hardly appreciates the decisive value of the military's inefficiency and incompetence in creating vast markets for civilian interests. In fact, the notion of an independent military sector, with its own codes and objectives, saves critical observers the trouble of viewing the nature of American power as a much larger integrated phenomenon. The military is a most conformist and pliable aspect of the power system, quite drably bureaucratic, and it serves the purposes of capitalists and politicians without much reticence.

While it is true the technicians of violence are an intrinsic part of American leadership, these men begin with and often play many other roles as well, and as I have already argued, these roles are primary and a greater revelation of their true function. The ideologists of expansion and militarism in the United States have, with rare exceptions, been civilians in the tradition of what Huntington calls neo-Hamiltonianism, and not since Alfred T. Mahan has a professional officer penned a respectable rationale for the enlargement of American might that reflected distinctive ideological assumptions. Indeed, what is most significant about neo-Hamiltonianism is its role as a justification for the political capitalism that was the most critical outcome of American liberal reform, and its affinity for classic international expansion and adventure abroad. The failure of any significant sector of the military openly to rally to such theories of the positive and predatory state at any time reveals mainly that the American military is nonideological, even when civilians formulate a seemingly appropriate frame of reference for it.

There have been no coups, no hints of physical insubordination, no serious general political-military alliances. The one possible exception, the MacArthur controversy of 1951, was essentially a case of heading off the obvious political aims of a man whose overweening personal ambition and conceit was a quality of personality rather than a spearhead for a military alliance or a distinctive policy orientation. And it was a general, who, as President in 1961, warned of the dangers of the "military-industrial complex" *and* the "scientific-technological elite," and reaffirmed the virtue of civilian supremacy. Even MacArthur ended his days as an articulate opponent of total war, calling for nuclear disarmament.

No later than November 1947 the Army quietly informed its leading generals that they could neither write nor speak in a manner that contradicted the existing government policy toward Russia or the United Nations, an admonition that it often repeated. Publicly, in subsequent years such figures as General Omar N. Bradley, then head of the Joint Chiefs of Staff, stated that the function of the military was to assume responsibility for a military policy adequate for the implementation of the national political criteria and goals which the President and his chosen advisers defined. It was in this context during the Truman Administration that the State Department became the leading single exponent of expanded military power and the construction of an H-bomb, with the responsible military men operating within given and more stringent budgetary assumptions. "The Army respects its civilian leadership and abstains from any involvement in politics," General Maxwell D. Taylor, Army Chief of Staff, wrote to his major officers in September 1955.[7] When General Matthew B. Ridgway published his iconoclastic memoir the following year, he only revealed an intense desire to permit his Service freedom to war with the Air Force and Navy for a larger portion of the military budget, and not to be subjected to some "politico-military" party line before the civilians made their final decisions, at which point ". . . they could expect completely loyal and diligent execution of those decisions."[8]

There are, of course, the much publicized but ultimately unrepresentative extremes in the military viewpoint. At the one pole is the view of the professional nonideological technician of death, which the then head of the Marine Corps, General David M. Shoup, expressed in a statement in 1961: "We're professional soldiers. We fight any enemy the President designates. We don't have to develop hate. We don't just keep talking communism. . . . You might build up a hate against one enemy and find yourself fighting another."[9] The other position, even less consequential, is the jingoist reaction which so alarmed liberals in 1961 when the press revealed that John Birch and similar reactionary notions were a part of a military education program on about a score of bases, or a small minority of the total. What was truly significant about the phenomenon was that it was not more widespread, perhaps much less than in high schools and newspapers, and that it revealed how far the military had gone to censor the eccentric, idiosyncratic, and reactionary speeches of some of its generals. Such revelations were useful, for the fierce statements of a few impotent professorial geopoliticians, and the minor officers who used them, made the Kennedy Administration look relatively moderate at a time when it was advocating a vast civil defense program and a conventional military build-up, and attempting to create a first-strike nuclear strategy that, combined or individually, constituted a truly irrational new course in the arms race.

The moral of the few incidents of which we know is that the Birchite General Walker and those like him are summarily forced from the military and government service if their superiors cannot bring them into line. During the barely undercover "preventive war" discussions of August 1950, when Secretary of the Navy Francis Mathews publicly called for ". . . instituting a war to compel cooperation for peace," only the fact that he was "very contrite" when the President called him in saved Mathews his post.[10] While Hanson Baldwin claimed Mathews really reflected the views of Secretary of Defense Louis Johnson, thus posing a military challenge to civilian authority, what was most consequential was that all the personalities involved until that time were civilians. When shortly thereafter the head of the Air War College publicly urged preventive war against Russia, the Pentagon suspended him from his command.[11]

The military, in brief, has been docile, its alleged "ethic" nebulous and meaningless. It has dissented no more than any other group of bureaucrats serving the state, and unquestionably it has been among the most restrained of those in power. A closer look at the manner in which the Military Establishment has operated only confirms this point.

The Military after the Second World War

The central fact of the immediate postwar experience is that although the American Military Establishment was more than sufficient in regard to what Washington considered to be the major military problem—the Soviet Union—it was relatively starved not merely in contrast to the potential of the American economy, but also when measured against the actual as opposed to the perceived global challenges to American power abroad. Nearly everyone in Washington saw the question of communism and the Left as essentially a matter of the Soviet Union and Europe, and not until 1949 and thereafter did the question of Asia assume sufficiently high priority to warrant a shift toward a slightly more balanced military capacity. In reality, the American political definition of the world's main "problems" served as a usefully reinforcing underpinning to an almost universal desire to limit the military budget, for if Russia was the primary opponent, the relatively low cost of the strategic atomic theory of the Air Force made sense. The significant point is that the Air Force atomic strategy, which Congress endorsed, made it possible to place a ceiling on arms expenditures, and only the rude events of Korea, Indo-China, and the gradual shift of American priorities from Europe to Asia and Latin America inevitably forced arms expenditures ever upward.

In this process of changing concerns, lasting from 1946 to the beginning of the "New Look" under Eisenhower, Service divisions over fundamental strategic assumptions left the civilians quite free to continue to make the critical decisions regarding the extent and use of military power. It is this profound disunity that is the central fact of the potential political role of the military in the United States, and it was especially sharp during the lean years of 1946–50, when the military budget ranged from a low of $11.8 billion in 1948, or 4.5 percent of the gross national product, to a high of $14.4 billion in 1947, 6.2 percent of the GNP. In the context of opposition to Truman's two-year efforts to unify the military services into a single Department of Defense, eventually embodied in the National Security Act of July 1947, the Navy had overtly opposed any move toward reducing the future role of sea power. Less openly, the Army hoped to save its weakened position against the Air Force, which claimed total capacity to deter or win a war with Russia cheaply, by advancing a Universal Military Training bill in Congress, a politically unpopular proposal that Truman also mildly endorsed. And to relate itself to military probabilities, the Navy advanced plans for supercarriers capable of delivering bombs against the Soviet heartland.

Since all these conflicting strategic and organizational claims carried substantial price tags, and Congress was unwilling to pay for them all, the more attractive doctrine and political connections of the Air Force prevailed. Congress, with the Air Force's assistance, killed U.M.T., and the Army passively watched while the advocates of air power in Congress undercut the Navy supercarrier program. By the spring of 1949, when the Secretary of the Navy resigned in protest over the course of events, both the Air Force and Navy were engaged in a propaganda war against each other, unquestionably the most interesting and artful in the history of American strategic doctrine.[12]

A number of officers of the tactical fighter section of the

Air Force, who resented the emphasis on big bombers, aided the Navy, but the furor over the B-36 bomber—on which the Air Force pinned its hopes for lack of a better plane—was the chief factor in strengthening the Navy's position. The Air Force's own experts privately had shown little enthusiasm for the B-36, which, with the aid of memos that Navy officers and competitive air frame producers distributed, correctly looked too much like an effort to bail out the sinking fortunes of the politically well-connected Consolidated Vultee Aircraft Company, whose links reached as high as Secretary of Defense Louis Johnson.[13] In the course of House hearings during October 1949 the Navy tendentiously advocated the value of carrier-based mobile air power and limited warfare, arguing the immorality of a city-busting atomic blitz as "morally reprehensible" and the illegal "mass killing of noncombatants." Such pleading was hollow, since the supercarrier was also useful mainly as a "city buster" against civilian populations. And as the Secretary of the Air Force, W. Stuart Symington maintained with greater consistency, the destruction of civilians is ". . . an unavoidable result of modern total warfare," and ". . . this opinion that war is immoral is a fairly recent one for anybody in the Military Establishment, and I wondered how and why it came up."[14]

No one in the Navy truly believed their moralistic contentions, and when eventually the Polaris submarine missile was invented, they too developed a strategic doctrine appropriate to that "city-busting" weapon. Truman was to fire at least one key Navy officer for his resistance to the official line, the Chief of Naval Operations, Admiral Louis E. Denfeld, and he disciplined others. What was at stake was not merely the independence of the various Services, but the belief, as General Bradley phrased it, that ". . . a nation's economy is its ultimate strength," and how they might obtain maximum security for the least expense remained the crucial issue.[15] Most of the Army generals who rose to prominence in the Joint Chiefs of Staff, as well as Herbert Hoover, Eisenhower, and the main forces of the budget-minded Republican Party, reinforced this assumption at the time. Congress itself has exerted control over the military not by aligning with it but rather by working within the President's broad guidelines and budgetary allocations to make certain that the Administration cut their constituents into as large a slice of the pie as possible. Other than this pork barrel impulse, which occasionally Congress translates into specific weapons systems that hardly alter the larger contours of the Executive branch's strategy, the role of Congress has merely been passively self-interested.[16]

If later the Army was to produce its own dissidents, the nature of the competitive struggle for limited budgetary resources in the 1950's meant that the profound divisions within the Military Establishment would always permit the civilians to play one Service bloc, consisting of the generals and their contractors, against the other. It is less significant to speculate what might have happened had the military assumed a common front, which is nearly impossible, than to realize that at no time did the political decision-makers lose control of the policy process.

America's civilian leaders applied the nation's policies within the informal and shifting committee-like structure that they organized into the National Security Council after mid-1947. United States leadership first defined those goals during the period 1896–1920, when McKinley, Roosevelt, and Wilson first scaled the objectives of American foreign policy to the capacity of American power to extend into the world. No later than the end of the Second World War those aims included a full-blown ideology of United States hegemony in the Western Hemisphere and Pacific, and primary leadership in the greater part of the areas that remained. Those goals reflected the American peace aims hammered out during the war, a process that excluded the Military Establishment on most of the key questions.

The very disunity within the military Services filled various key leaders in Washington with suspicion toward the consistency and reliability of the new Department of Defense, and they learned to depend on their own resources within the National Security Council and other committees. Although the original Council included the three Service secretaries, these men were all civilians; and while the Joint Chiefs attended meetings during the first years of the Council's existence, not until after the Korean War did they participate in the Council's vital staff functions. During 1949 Truman dropped the Service secretaries, and after the Korean War sharply cut back on the size of Council meetings, and the Defense Department has largely restricted itself to technical advice and analysis of the military implications of foreign policy decisions of the President, Secretary of State, or the advisers that the President uses informally. If Cabinet agencies set up independent planning committees from time to time, meshing foreign and military policy, the Executive ultimately considered their recommendations in a manner that lowers the relative weight of Defense and military opinion. The Government, for the most part, has not determined basic foreign policy otherwise.[17]

Significantly, the civilians rather than the military attempted to break out of the traditional straitjacket of budgetary limitations to attain a force level equal to American political goals and ideological conceptions. During 1949 George Kennan argued for greater emphasis on mobile conventional armies. And it was with the budgetary restriction in mind that Dean Acheson, David Lilienthal, and Louis Johnson urged the President in January 1950 to authorize preliminary studies on the H-bomb, a weapon most of Washington then considered necessary in light of the Soviet discovery of the secret of making an A-bomb, to retain military superiority within a limited budget. The State Department, developing Kennan's original impulse and making it more grandiose, at the same time took the lead in a joint Defense-State committee to urge a vast increase in the military budget, which the State Department proposed to make between $35–50 billion, tying it to general ideological descriptions of the communist menace. The Joint Chiefs and Defense leaders, more modest and less ideological, and split within their own ranks due to Secretary Johnson's desire to cut the Defense budget, could propose only $17–18 billion, a modest increase over existing levels. At this juncture the Korean War began, with the conflicting positions in the policy paper now known as JCS 68 still unresolved.

By 1953 the military budget had grown to 13.8 percent of the gross national product, but in the White House a former general undertook to reduce the percentage with his "New Look" military policy of greater reliance on nuclear power. Eisenhower was concerned with the problem of how to maintain vast military power over a long period of time without overheating the nonmilitary economic sector and without assuming, as had the Democrats, that the danger of war with Russia increased with growing Soviet military and economic power. Above all, he wished to confront the extraordinarily difficult and ultimately unresolvable dilemma of how to combat or neutralize the diverse social revolutionary threats to the permanent strategic, political, and economic goals of the United States—a dilemma which has characterized American foreign policy since the fall of China. America's capacity to confront successfully the Soviet Union required a budgetary expenditure and strategic posture that was predictable. However, such a policy was inadequate to meet the challenge of the many, often yet unborn local revolutionary situations, where crude weapons made strategic nuclear weaponry inappropriate and potentially suicidal. America's economic and political limitations could not halt a world drifting beyond its control.

Ultimately, the Eisenhower Administration chose to confront Russia and to risk its ability effectively to respond militarily to the rest of the world. The General and his government rejected a full mobilization of American manpower and economic resources into a total warfare state capable of seriously retarding revolutionary movements everywhere. The result was a doctrine of massive retaliation appropriate for warfare against highly industrialized powers, which the Government now frankly acknowledges as unlikely, and a beginning in the long-term decline in the coveted American hegemony in the world. The upshot, too, has been that in the rare instances which tempted factions of the military to use nuclear weapons, such as in Indo-China during the spring of 1954, the Army's fundamental skepticism toward this strategy made employment of it impossible. Under the New Look policy, the absolute and percentage decline in military expenditures and Army-Navy manpower continued, much to the disgust of Army generals, until Kennedy came to office. In effect, military policy and outlays were sufficient only to maintain a high level of economic activity at home, but insufficient to cope with social revolution and guerrilla warfare, against which missiles and atomic weapons were largely useless.[18]

The "Civilianized" Military

Within the context of these internal military divisions, the Services' lack of a unified strategic doctrine, and the overriding limits of the budgetary process in defining options, it would be difficult to prove C. Wright Mills' contention that ". . . as a coherent group of men the military is probably the most competent now concerned with national policy; no other group has had the training in co-ordinated economic, political, and military affairs. . . ."[19] On the contrary, nothing in the operational structure of the Defense Establishment nor in the changing character of military technology alters the fact that civilian, even "liberal," leadership and civilian ideology have led the United States and the world into its present morass of global crises and interventionism.

Each successive reorganization of the Defense Establishment since 1947 has further consolidated the decisive role of civilians in military policy. In 1949 Congress deprived the Services of independent executive status and placed over it a Defense Department structure with superior powers. In one of his first and most critical acts, the stronger civilian Secretary created an independent, superior office to control all missile developments within the three Services, thereby dominating the most essential sector of future military technology. The Defense Reorganization Act of 1953 further accelerated the civilian domination of the Defense Department by increasing the number of civilian assistant secretaries from three to nine and assigning them many responsibilities hitherto left to civilian-military boards. While certain of their functions were vague, it placed larger control of functional problems in the hands of civilians who were not responsible to the Services but to the Defense Secretary. One of them, indeed, represented unified Defense policy on international affairs directly to the National Security Council. In this context, with the three services so profoundly divided on strategy and in competition for limited budgetary resources which the civilians could use to split their ranks, the Joint Chiefs of Staff were unable to stem the supremacy of the civilians in the Pentagon. The President usually selected a politically reliable officer to be the head of the Joint Chiefs, and the Air Force was more than willing to break away from the other Services at the sacrifice of a possible common front because, in the showdown, it usually could better protect its own interests against the others. When united, which meant primarily on minor questions, the civilian leaders treated the Joint Chiefs deferentially. In any event, the Defense Reorganization Act of 1958 further strengthened the role of the civilian secretaries, and in that year the Secretary, via the Advanced Research Projects Agency, took over responsibility for all important weapons systems developments.[20]

In the context of the ever-growing dependence of the professional soldiers on the civilian Defense Secretaries, both the soldiers and civilians in the Pentagon in turn increased their reliance on the civilians in business and the universities for the major technological innovations and strategies which are the most grotesquely threatening aspect of the arms race and the condition of the world today. The fact was that the generals and admirals were incapable of managing and developing scientifically sophisticated "hardware" programs with which the United States hoped to compensate for its manpower and ideological disadvantages in a revolutionary world. Most, indeed, were near illiterates in the major critical areas, and alone were patently unable to attain the maximum military impact and resources from the budgets that Congress had allocated. Conscious of these limitations, in 1946 Eisenhower had decided for the Army that ". . . there appears little reason for duplicating within the Army an outside organization which by its experience is better qualified than we are to carry out some of our tasks," which meant the Army would ". . . find much of the talent we need for comprehensive planning in industry and universities."[21] Thus began a vast research and development program and military dependence on industry and universities, and an even larger stake on the part of a vital sector of these institutions in an arms race. In 1948 the Air Force took over the Rand Corporation on contract to secure its advice, and from 1953 to 1958 relied for the direction of its missile program on the Ramo-Wooldridge Corporation, whose ballistic missile staff grew from 18 to 3,269 in five years. After 1953 the Air Force left the co-ordination of its specific weapons systems to its prime con-tractors, and by 1959 drew 46 percent of its procurement personnel at the supervisory level from private business back-grounds—a figure the Navy and Army almost matched. In the field of missiles almost all of the government's key advisers have been civilians from industry and the universities. By 1955 the Pentagon's in-house Weapons System Evaluation Group was near collapse, and only a contract between M.I.T. and the Defense Department, which led to the creation of the multi-university-sponsored Institute for Defense Analysis, saved that undertaking—but in civilian, private hands.[22] By the time the Kennedy Administration took office, civilians had so thoroughly permeated the Military Establishment with their techniques, ideology, and objectives that it was apparent that professional officers were hardly more than docile instruments of the state, less credible to its civilian leadership than even many facile and ambitious Ivy League Ph.D.'s who, in their ability to translate American power into strategies and arms systems, saw the opportunity of becoming advisers to the men already at the top.

The final reorganization of the Defense Department, which Robert McNamara merely completed, utterly depersonalized the distinctive aspects of a military bureaucracy on the premise ". . . that the techniques used to administer these affairs of a large organization are very similar whether that organization be a business enterprise or a Government institution, or an educational institution, or any other large aggregation of human individuals working to a common end."[23] In reality, McNamara's model and experience was the Ford Motor Com-pany, but in the Defense Department he sought to maximize objectives at the lowest possible price rather than accumulate an annual profit. Ph.D.'s managed the resulting "package pro-

grams" and increasingly centralized procurement at the further expense of the professional soldiers, who whimpered
bitterly but continued to lose vital leverage and administrative
functions. Complaints from the generals still often centered
on the matter of budgetary allocations for the various Services,
or their deflated egos and the roles of officers in ever-narrow-
ing areas, but they did not alter the essential reality of the
further "civilianization" of the commanding sectors of the
Military Establishment, mainly in the hands of political "liberals" dedicated to civil rights, social welfare, and art centers
which have become the liberal's surrogates for a society based
on economic foundations of justice.[24]

The collapse of the McNamara empire did not end civilian
predominance, even as these civilians chose the new generation of generals more for their technical competence than
their military prowess. As a materialist *par excellence,* Mc-
Namara eventually realized that the unattainable ideological
goals of American policy had outstripped physical resources,
turning the war in Vietnam into a seemingly endless series of
escalations, each one only further intensifying the defeats
America was suffering in the hands of peasants. His elimination came not from his disagreements with the military but
with the other civilians who were even more belligerent than
he had been throughout his career. Indeed, this episode perhaps more than any other exposed how totally military in
means and ends were the ideological premises of those who
believed also in the supremacy of civilian authority over the
military. It showed how fully the Military Establishment was
merely the instrument of warfare liberalism in the Fair Deal-
Great Society period of American history. And Vietnam, in
turn, revealed how irrelevant the ingenuity and technical efficiency of American policy had been in a Third World whose
fate revolutionary mass movements would determine, despite
resistance, repression, and occasional setbacks.

THE UNITED STATES

AND WORLD ECONOMIC POWER

THERE IS NO COMPREHENSIVE THEORY of the contemporary world crisis. That both conventional academic or Left scholars have failed or been unable to assess the causes and meaning of the most significant events of our time in large part reflects their unwillingness to confront directly the nature of American interest and power. Theories of imperialism are now the dry-as-dust topics of academic tomes, and all too few have made a serious effort to scratch beneath the ideology of American expansion to define its larger needs, imperatives, and functions as a system.

Earlier studies of imperialism left no doubt as to what one had to examine in order to comprehend the role of a state in the world. Whether it was imperialist rivalries for economic and strategic power, the atavism of feudal ideologies, reaction and counterrevolution, or the desire to integrate and stabilize a world economy, the study of foreign policy was specific, real, and discounted the notion of error, myth, and exuberance as the sources of conduct as explanations sufficient only for national patriots. American scholars have not translated their ability to perceive correctly the roots of diplomacy in the past into a description of contemporary American policy, even though the same categories and analogies may be equally relevant today.

To understand the unique economic interests and aspirations of the United States in the world, and the degree to which it benefits or loses within the existing distribution and structure of power and the world economy, is to define a crucial basis for comprehending as well as predicting its role overseas. The nature of the international crisis, and the limited American responses to it, tell us why the United States is in Vietnam and why in fact American intervention inevitably colors the direction of the vast changes in the world political and social system which are the hallmarks of modern history. In brief, the manner in which the United States has expanded its problems and objectives overseas, transforming the American crisis into a global one, also explains its consistent interventionism.

It is critical, as part of a comprehensive theory of the world crisis, to study the control and organization of the international economy, who gains and who loses in it, and how we have arrived at the present impasse. We should neither dismiss nor make too much of the issue of ideology or the less systematic belief, as former Secretary of Defense James Forrestal once put it, that ". . . our security is not merely the capacity or ability to repel invasion, it is our ability to contribute to the reconstruction of the world. . . ."[1] For American ideology is a vague synthesis that embodies, once its surface is scratched, economic and strategic objectives and priorities that a thin rhetoric rationalizes into doctrines more interesting for what they imply than for what they state. For purposes of this chapter I shall deal only with the structure and the material components of the world economy that set the context for the repeated local interventions and crises that are the major characteristics of the modern world scene.

The United States and Raw Materials

The role of raw materials is qualitative rather than merely quantitative, and neither volume nor price can measure their ultimate significance and consequences. The economies and technologies of the advanced industrial nations, the United States in particular, are so intricate that the removal of even a small part, as in a watch, can stop the mechanism. The steel industry must add approximately thirteen pounds of manganese to each ton of steel, and though the weight and value of the increase is a tiny fraction of the total, a modern diversified steel industry *must* have manganese. The same analogy is true of the entire relationship between the industrial and so-called developing nations: The nations of the Third World may be poor, but in the last analysis the industrial world needs their resources more than these nations need the West, for poverty is nothing new to peasantry cut off from export sectors, and trading with industrial states has not ended their subsistence living standards. In case of a total rupture between the industrial and supplier nations, it is the population of the industrial world that proportionately will suffer the most.

Since the Second World War the leaders of the United States have been acutely aware of their vital reliance on raw materials, and the fact, to quote Paul G. Hoffman, former Marshall Plan administrator, that ". . . our own dynamic economy has made us dependent on the outside world for many critical raw materials."[2] Successive Administrations have been incessantly concerned over the ability and necessity of the United States to develop these resources everywhere, given the paucity of local capital and technology, and their interest extends far beyond short-term profits of investment.

In areas such as Africa this obsession has defined American policy on every major issue.

At the beginning of this century the United States was a net earner in the export of minerals and commodities, but by 1926–30 it had a vast annual deficit of crude materials, and in 1930 imported 5 percent of its iron ore, 64 percent of its bauxite (aluminum), 65 percent of its copper, 9 percent of its lead, and 4 percent of its zinc. Imports of these five critical metals by 1960 had increased to 32 percent for iron ore, 98 percent for bauxite, 35 percent for lead, and 60 percent for zinc, and only in the case of copper declined to 46 percent. As a percentage of the new supply, the United States in 1956 imported at least 80 percent of thirty-nine necessary commodities, 50 to 79 percent of fifteen commodities, 10 to 49 percent of twenty commodities, and less than 10 percent of another twenty-three—all with a total import value of $6.6 billion. There was no doubt, as one Senate report concluded in 1954, that Washington knew that should the mineral-rich nations cut off these sources, "To a very dangerous extent, the vital security of this Nation is in serious jeopardy."[3]

By 1956–60 the United States was importing over half of all its required metals and almost 60 percent of its wool. It imported all tropical foodstuffs, such as cocoa, coffee, and bananas, as well as over half the sugar supply. When, in 1963, Resources for the Future completed its monumental survey of raw materials and projected American needs for the next forty years, it predicted a vast multiplication of American demands that made imperative, in its estimate, ". . . that in the future even larger amounts of certain items will have to be drawn from foreign sources if demand is to be satisfied without marked increases in cost."[4] Its medium projections suggested immensely increased needs for nearly all metals, ranging as high as nine times for molybdenum to about two and one-half times for lead. Within three years, however, all of the critical output, consumption, and population assumptions upon which the Resources for the Future experts based their speculations proved to be far too conservative, the omnivorous demands of the economy were far greater than they had expected.

A critical shift in the location of the world's most vital mineral output and reserves has accompanied the imperative need for raw materials in the United States. In 1913 the developing nations accounted for 3 percent of the world's total iron ore output and 15 percent of its petroleum, as opposed to 37 percent and 65 percent, respectively, in 1965. Its share of bauxite output increased from 21 percent in 1928 to 69 percent in 1965. The United States share of world oil output fell from 61 percent in 1938 to 29 percent in 1964, as the known world reserves shifted toward the Middle East.

Despite the introduction of synthetics between 1938 and 1954, which reduced by about one-fifth the quantity of natural raw materials needed for the average constant quantity of goods produced in the industrial nations, the vast increase in world industrial output has more than compensated for the shift and greatly increased pressures on raw materials supplies from the industrial nations. In effect, the United States has become more dependent on imported raw materials as its share of the consumption of the world's total has declined sharply in the face of European and Japanese competition for supplies. The United States, which consumed slightly less than half of the world's total output of copper, lead, zinc, aluminum, and steel in 1948–50, consumed slightly over one-quarter in 1960, save for aluminum, where the percentage decline was still great. This essentially European demand, which has grown far more rapidly than in the United States, has challenged the American predominance in the world raw materials trade in a manner which makes the maintenance and expansion of existing sources in the ex-colonial regions doubly imperative to it.[5]

American and European industry can find most of these future sources of supply, so vital to their economic growth, only in the continents in upheaval and revolution. Over half of United States iron ore imports in 1960 came from Venezuela and three equally precarious Latin American countries. Over half the known world reserves of manganese are in Russia and China, and most of the remainder is in Brazil, India, Gabon, and South Africa. South Africa and Rhodesia account for nearly all the world's chromium reserves, Cuba and New Caledonia for half the nickel, China for over two-thirds the tungsten, and Chile, Northern Rhodesia, Congo, and Peru for well over two-thirds of the foreign copper reserves. Guyana has about six times the American reserves of bauxite, and China has three times, while Malaya, Indonesia, and Thailand alone have two-thirds the world tin reserves, with Bolivia and the Congo possessing most of the balance. Only zinc and lead, among the major metals, are in politically stable regions, from the American viewpoint.[6]

It is extraordinarily difficult to estimate the potential role and value of these scarce minerals to the United States, but certain approximate definitions are quite sufficient to make the point that the future of American economic power is too deeply involved for this nation to permit the rest of the world to take its own political and revolutionary course in a manner that imperils the American freedom to use them. Suffice it to say, the ultimate significance of the importation of certain critical raw materials is not their cost to American business but rather the end value of the industries that *must* employ these materials, even in small quantities, or pass out of existence. And in the larger sense, confident access to raw materials is a necessary precondition for industrial expansion into new or existing fields of technology, without the fear of limiting shortages which the United States' sole reliance on its national resources would entail. Intangibly, it is really the political and psychological assurance of total freedom of development of national economic power that is vital to American economic growth. Beyond this, United States profits abroad are made on overseas investments in local export industries, giving the Americans the profits of the suppliers as well as the consumer. An isolated America would lose all this, and much more.

It is not enough, therefore, to state that nonfood raw materials imports doubled in value between 1953 and 1966, and that $16.6 billion in imports for the food and industrial users in 1966 was vitally necessary to American prosperity. More relevant is the fact that in 1963 the Census valued the iron and steel industry's shipments at $22.3 billion, the aluminum's at $3.9 billion, metal cans at $2.1 billion, copper at $3.1 billion, asbestos at a half billion, zinc at a half billion, coffee at $1.9 billion, sugar and chocolate at $1.7 billion—and that all of these industries and many others, to some critical extent, depended on their access to the world's supply of raw materials. Without the availability of such goods for decades, at prices favorable to the United States, the American economy would have been far different—and much poorer.

To suggest that the United States could solve its natural shortages by attempting to live within its raw materials limits would also require a drastic reduction in its exports of finished goods, and this the leaders of the American system would never voluntarily permit, for it would bring profound economic repercussions for a capitalist economy in the form of vast unemployment and lower profits. While only four or five percent of American steel mill products went to exports in 1955–60, this proportion reached nearly one-quarter in the aluminum and one-fifth in the copper industries. In this context the United States has become a processor of the world's raw materials in a number of fields not simply to satisfy domestic needs but also its global export trade and military ambitions. At home, a policy of self-sufficiency would, in the case of aluminum, seriously affect the building construction industry, consumer and producer durables, and transport industries. The same is true for copper, which is critical for producer durables, building construction, communications, and electric power. Minor metals, of which the United States is largely deficient, are essential to any technologically advanced nation, especially to the chemical, electrical, and electronics industries.[7]

America's ability to procure at will such materials as it needs, and at a price it can afford, is one of the keystones of its economic power in this century. The stakes are vast, and its capacity to keep intact something like the existing integrated but unequal relations between the poor, weak nations and the United States is vital to the future of its mastery of the international economy.

The United States and World Exports

The dominant interest of the United States is in world economic stability, and anything that undermines that condition presents a danger to its present hegemony. Countering, neutralizing and containing the disturbing political and social trends thus becomes the most imperative objective of its foreign policy.

For the developing nations, the postwar experience has been one of relative decline in world commerce, a pattern that has vastly benefited the industrial nations of Europe and the United States, who have done almost nothing to alter a situation that has greatly favored their own economies. No matter what the source, all agree that since 1948 the overall share of the developing nations in the world export trade has decreased consistently, the specific aspects and causes of this reduction deserving more detail later in this chapter. Taking the United Nations data, from 1950 to 1966 the share of the developing nations in world exports fell from 31.2 percent to 19.1 percent. Latin America suffered worst in this regard.[8] Though the absolute value of the exports of developing nations had steadily increased, it has been at a much slower growth rate than among industrial nations, where, in turn, the Common Market nations and Japan, long after their wartime recovery, have not only consistently and greatly outstripped the developing nations, but Great Britain and the United States as well. Moreover, just as the industrialized nations have shared more of their export trade among themselves, the Common Market nations have set the pace by trading among themselves to an unprecedented degree. They have collectively displaced the United States as the major importer from the Third World and since 1953 have almost equaled the United States in exports to these nations.

In 1954–56 the United States accounted for 30.5 percent of the world export trade for principal manufactures, by 1961 had slipped to 25.3 percent, and in 1966 to 22.7 percent. Given the faster growth rate in exports of goods such as machinery and transport equipment, processed food, beverages, and highly finished articles, the exceptional success of the Common Market nations in intra-Market trade, Africa, and especially Latin America has meant the gradual weakening of United States power in the world manufacturing export market and the re-emergence of Europe as a major, viable competitor with the United States in classic, traditional capitalist terms.[9] West Europe is succeeding, as well, in carving out an even larger share of the trade of the Third World, where the United States proportion of exports has significantly declined, reducing the magnitude of American access to vital raw materials.

At the same time that the United States has been losing in competition against the other major capitalist industrialized nations as an exporter of manufactures, its relationship to the Third World for control of the world trade in agricultural commodities indicates a long-term pattern of American success at the expense of the poorer countries. For the United States is not only a highly industrialized nation, consuming raw materials, but its immense agricultural output requires it to sell ever-growing quantities of food abroad, closing possible markets and earnings to developing nations. America's agricultural exports grew from $2.9 billion in 1950 to $6.9 billion in 1966, its agricultural imports increasing only by one-eighth during that period.

While it is difficult to estimate the extent to which the vast increase of United States shares in world exports of certain foods, such as wheat, was due to temporary relief, it is certain that for two decades the active, aggressive export expansion of the agricultural sector has been a fundamental American policy having little to do with humanitarian concerns. It has often contributed to world gluts within the market economy and lower Third World earnings, bringing the poor nations, ultimately, more misery. Table III illustrates the increase of the United States share of the world agricultural export market, generally far in excess of the American share of world production. Briefly, it reveals that the highly commercial American policy in agriculture, which resulted in the export of 42 percent of its rice, and one-third its wheat and cotton output in 1954–58, led to a critical and unprecedented American domination of the world agricultural food and cotton trade. Even more important, if we calculate the United States share of the total world agricultural export trade, from 1953 to 1966 it increased from 12 to 19 percent, significantly offsetting America's loss to Europe in the manufacturing trade market.[10]

TABLE III

UNITED STATES SHARE IN WORLD EXPORTS
AND PRODUCTION OF SELECTED AGRICULTURAL PRODUCTS
1934–35, 1955–57, AND 1965

	Percentage Share in World Exports			Percentage Share in World Production		
	1934–35	1955–57	1965	1934–35	1955–57	1965
Wheat	6.4	46.1	38.0	21.0	20.2	14.5
Oats	5.9	29.3	19.4	31.0	37.1	29.7
Corn	9.0	63.9	60.6	59.3	59.2	45.7
Rice	.8	14.8	21.7	1.0	1.8	1.4
Cotton	43.0	43.6	27.0*	51.9	35.5	20.2*
Tobacco	41.0	37.6	45.0	30.2	32.3	20.5
Soybeans	2.3	82.0	89.1	9.5	51.3	63.0

* 1966

Calculated from data in U.S. Senate, Committee on Foreign Relations, *United States-Latin American Relations.* ["Compilation of Studies"] 86:2. August 31, 1960 (Washington, 1960), 452; United Nations, Statistical Office, *Statistical Yearbook, 1966* (New York, 1967); U.S. Department of Agriculture, *Handbook of Agricultural Charts, 1967* (Washington, 1967), and monthly issues of *World Agricultural Production and Trade;* Food and Agricultural Organization of the United Nations, *Trade Yearbook, 1966* (Rome, 1967).

It is within this larger setting—American losses to Europe in the industrial export sector, dependence on the raw materials of the developing world, and mastery over the developing nations in many world agricultural exports—that Washington pursues its foreign policy. The details of these economic relationships and their causes reveal more fully the purposes and objectives of America in the world today.

World Trade and World Misery

If the postwar experience is any indication, the nonsocialist developing nations have precious little reason to hope that they can terminate the vast misery of their masses. For in reality the industrialized nations have increased their advantages over them in the world economy by almost any standard one might care to use.

The terms of trade—the unit value or cost of goods a region imports compared to its exports—have consistently disfavored the developing nations since 1958, ignoring altogether the fact that the world prices of raw materials prior to that time were never a measure of equity. Using 1958 as a base year, by 1966 the value of the exports of developing areas had fallen to 97, those of the industrial nations had risen to 104. Using the most extreme example of this shift, from 1954 to 1962 the terms of trade deteriorated 38 percent against the developing nations, for an income loss in 1962 of about $11 billion, or 30 percent more than the financial aid the Third World received that year. Even during 1961–66, when the terms of trade remained almost constant, their loss in potential income was $13.4 billion, wiping away 38 percent of the income from official foreign aid plans of every sort.

Since about one-half the exports of the developing countries are mining products, and about two-fifths agricultural, fishery, and forestry products, the comparative patterns in the prices and output of these goods reveal somewhat more.

The developing nations' food export prices have fallen, particularly coffee and sugar, for an overall decline of 7 percent between 1950–54 and 1961–65. Nonfood agricultural prices fell 9 percent during that time, but the price of minerals and fuels rose only 3 percent—together, the decline has spelled greater misery for the Third World.

The developing nations have compensated for this price decrease by exporting 60 percent more in 1966 than 1958, as opposed to an 87 percent increase for the industrialized nations. The result was a serious reduction in their share of world trade. But minerals and petroleum accounted for much of the increase in quantity, with an absolute quantity decline on types of nonfood agriculture. In effect, relatively inflexible demand for certain foods, the introduction of synthetic textiles, rubber, and the like, and the rising prices of industrial goods contributed to the already groaning problems of the developing world. All of this has revealed once more that rather than the existence of a harmony between the rich and poor nations, the drift of affairs and, as we shall see, Western policies have led to a further aggravation of the condition of the majority of the world's peoples.[11]

In fact, whether intended or otherwise, low prices and economic stagnation in the Third World directly benefit the industrialized nations. Should the developing nations ever industrialize to the extent that they begin consuming a significant portion of their own oil and mineral output, they would reduce the available supply to the United States and prices would rise. And there has never been any question that conservative American studies of the subject have treated the inability of the Third World to industrialize seriously as a cause for optimism in raw materials planning. Their optimism is fully warranted, since nations dependent on the world market for the capital to industrialize are unlikely to succeed, for when prices of raw materials are high they tend to concentrate on selling more raw materials, and when prices are low their earnings are insufficient to raise capital for diversification. The United States especially gears its investments, private and public, to increasing the output of exportable minerals and agricultural commodities, instead of balanced economic development. With relatively high capital-labor intensive investment and feeding transport facilities to port areas rather than to the population, such investments hardly scratch the living standards of the great majority of the local peasantry or make possible the large increases in agricultural output that are a precondition of a sustained industrial expansion. Indeed, the total flow of private and public foreign capital to the developing areas, amounting to $10.1 billion in 1965, has only increased the output of resources needed in the Western world, and the flight of local capital toward safe Western banks has partially offset even this form of capital influx.

Taking the value of world manufacturing produced in the developing areas, after a period of decline, the share of this region in 1961 finally attained its 1938 portion of 9.3 percent of the world's manufacturing output, excluding Russia and East Europe. If we add mining, a function of service mainly to the industrial states, then between 1938 and 1961 the proportion increased from 9.9 percent to 11.3 percent. In terms of the world's gross domestic product, the developing nations' share declined from 17.6 percent to 17.4 percent over this period, while their percentage of the population grew from 67.3 to 70.3. Stagnation, therefore, has been the primary characteristic of the Third World.

A closer look at the data, however, reveals that the developing countries have remained essentially agricultural even where annual manufacturing growth is substantial, in part because foreign investments have been capital intensive and employ fewer workers, and also because light manufacturing still predominates in these instances. In terms of world export trade, the developing nations tend to trade with each other for such manufactures as they may produce, and if we remove Hong Kong and Israel from the calculations as two most untypical examples, the share of Third World manufactured products in international trade drops dramatically. What is much more significant is that despite modest increases in absolute output, per capita food production in the Third World between 1934–38 and 1961–65 declined in Africa and Latin America and remained static in the Far and Near East. Between 1958–59 and 1963–64 the per capita food consumption in Latin America fell a drastic 7 percent. Another measure of this trend, the average income per inhabitant in the noncommunist developing nations and the noncommunist industrial sector, reveals a ratio of inequality of about one to six in 1900 and one to twelve in 1965.[12]

Dual Standard Policy

Although the United States for over two decades has advocated that all nations sharply lower their tariffs and rely on a world economy of essentially free trade, it has never been willing to implement this policy when it was not to the interest of powerful American industries. This American refusal to open fully its own economy to the world, which would undoubtedly gain thereby, is the vital difference between a desire to dominate the world economy—a new imperialism—and a theory of free trade or the "Open Door." The net effect of this dual standard has been to enlarge United States economic power in the Third World and partially to stem the decisive advantages that West Europe increasingly holds in the industrial sector. For since 1949, when the United States refused to ratify an International Trade Organization it had initiated, everyone understood that the United States would advocate one economic doctrine for the rest of the world merely as a pretense for mastering the world economy to the maximum extent possible—but at the same time practice another code itself.

The United States maintains import quotas and tariff barriers on agricultural products and minerals in order to sustain high prices for its own producers, while simultaneously depriving Third World nations of an export market they could probably command in at least several critical fields.

In 1960 the United States had quotas and tariffs on nine Third World products, including petroleum, sugar, and cotton, and while it removed restrictions from zinc and lead at the end of 1965, the possibility of reimposing them remains. An effective "sanitary" embargo on live cattle and dressed beef and veal also existed, while Congress placed tariffs on many other agricultural and primary products. There is no way a nation can export a sack of sugar to the United States if Congress has not already allocated a quota to it under the Sugar Act, which reserves a majority of the quota for United States producers and the Philippines, where American owners dominate the industry. "The agricultural export sales policies and the import quotas on minerals," one leading United States trader warned President Eisenhower in 1958, "put the United States in the role of perhaps the world's greatest violator of the principles that it advocates in international competition and tries to sell to others through GATT."[13]

Changes in domestic programs for sugar, cotton, and oil within the United States, and to a lesser degree Europe, profoundly influence the sales and prices of Third World exports. United States price supports for cotton, for example, have helped determine plantings in Latin American nations, and extensive United States self-sufficiency in both oil and sugar has been a major loss of income to developing states. Latin American and Japanese exporters have for many years publicly complained, and the Latins have threatened retaliation, but for a variety of compelling economic reasons connected with the United States loan and investment program have been unable to implement their menacing words. In brief, the United States has attempted to maintain the most convenient aspects of both protectionism and free trade. For to have opened its doors to foreign agricultural surpluses and oil on a free market basis merely to be ideologically consistent would have resulted in enormous damage to America's coveted supremacy in the world economy.

The United States has been able to obtain its share of world agricultural exports, thwart retaliation, open needed raw materials supplies, and prevent an even more rapid decline in the share of manufacturing exports through adroitly using its foreign aid and loans to the world. Even before the Marshall Plan in 1947 the United States was ready to make foreign aid useful to itself by introducing ever greater emphasis on its value in developing raw materials sources and stockpiles the United States might someday need. The Foreign Assistance Act of 1948 (the Marshall Plan) required that aid recipients make at least 5 percent of the local "counterpart" currencies available to the United States to purchase raw materials, as well as open the European nations and their colonies to American investors on an equal basis. And between 1945 and 1951 the percentage of Export-Import Bank loans devoted to developing new foreign supplies of raw materials increased from 6 to 30 percent. By mid-1953 United States counterpart funds purchased $115 million in raw materials for American use, plus a larger amount in United States dollar purchases for direct stockpiling after the Korean War.

These policies were not exceptional, for raw materials guided every aspect of American policy toward the Third World, and the keystone of the Point Four program from 1950 onward was the accelerated expansion of world raw materials supplies and sources. In the case of India, which after the 1948 Russian embargo on manganese exports became the major available source of supply, Congress quickly made loans for grain and other needs contingent on repayment in manganese and other minerals, and although the final loan terms moderated the bluntness of some congressional enthusiasts, manganese as a factor in Indian-American economic relations became the basis of a vital *quid pro quo*. Congressmen frankly stated the reasons for this policy: "Manganese today is far more important to us . . . because it is used in the production of steel. We have to have it," as one North Carolina member phrased it. More bluntly, a Pittsburgh congressman made it plain that "We use tremendous quantities of manganese in the steel industry . . . and if we do not get this strategic material, our mills and our economy will shut down."[14]

The Americans got their Indian manganese, and using Point Four and the Export-Import Bank they later opened up Brazilian supplies during the 1950's as well. The various Administrations and Congresses consistently geared the bulk of American foreign aid funds to this function throughout the world, making the Third World more dependent on the needs and inconsistencies of the industrial nations, the United States in particular. "Not for one minute," John Foster Dulles told Congress in 1958 concerning one foreign aid proposal, "do I think the purpose . . . is to make friends. The purpose . . . is to look out for the interests of the United States."[15]

Another example of this assumption, and the manner in which it has operated to the detriment of Third World nations, was the raw materials stockpiling program which began in 1946 and accelerated after the Korean War. By the end of 1961 the United States Government had spent $8.9 billion and eventually found it had, in effect, also undertaken a partial subsidy program for domestic producers. When the Kennedy Administration sought to begin discarding vast holdings that far exceeded amounts required for national emergencies, it soon found it was having a depressing effect on world prices, especially on tin. As the United States Government quickly learned, it had also developed a means of hedging against higher raw materials prices, a fact that only helped keep the value of Third World exports at a lower level.[16]

★

The long standing opposition of the United States to commodity agreements which would stabilize at a high level the rapidly and continuously fluctuating prices of many of the world's key raw materials has been no less significant. This opposition, which dates back to the 1920's, reflects America's practice of maximizing its wealth by buying as cheaply as possible while it dumps agricultural goods on the world market and restricts imports damaging to its own producers. To the developing nations, price stability is the most attractive, fastest, and simplest means to increase their foreign exchange. In Latin America, for example, during 1960–63 nine minerals and agricultural commodities provided 70 percent of the foreign exchange earnings, the prices of most of them vacillating wildly as a matter of course. These fluctuations have vast significance, for a one-cent-a-pound increase in coffee could mean $65 million a year additional income to the exporting countries, or $100 million for rice producers—and increased costs to the American consumers. Since foreign aid and investment of every variety provide slightly more than one-tenth of the foreign exchange receipts of developing nations, their ability to raise and sustain the prices of such exportable assets as they have is the heart of any effective development program. Quite as significant, of course, is the internal redistribution of income via land reform and the elimination of United States investments in those export sectors that would obtain higher earnings.

Under these circumstances, effective commodity agreement programs would have a far-reaching impact on the distribution of the world's income and living standards. Experts conservatively estimated that a moderate world commodity program for coffee, tea, cocoa, sugar, and bananas in 1961 alone could have added $700 million to the incomes of the producer nations. Quite apart from the fact that such agreements would partially benefit American overseas investors in those fields as well, for whatever its motives the United States Government has always managed to oppose such comprehensive regulation of the vital minerals and agricultural goods it needs. This fact has contributed greatly to the high American standard of living.

Because the United States opposed the commodity agreements provisions that the developing nations offered at the International Trade Organization conference in 1948, the Charter was watered down to impotence, but Congress still refused to ratify it. Later that year the United States delegation entered a reservation on the subject at the Bogotá Conference, voted against a similar resolution at the Caracas Conference in 1954, abstained at another that year, issued another reservation at the Buenos Aires Conference of 1957, opposed a strong O.A.S. position, and in general has as tactfully as possible thwarted the desire of Latin American and other nations to earn more for their exports.

The United States has seen the dependence of the developing world on income from such raw materials as an opportunity to open the doors of those nations to increased investment and force greater output. "While we do not believe that commodity agreements, in general, serve the objective of obtaining more efficient production and distribution," the United States delegate to the February 1959 hemispheric conference declared, ". . . we recognize that they may serve temporarily . . . on a commodity-by-commodity basis."[17] Such temporary expediencies have served more to thwart the dangerous potential of the agreements and protect the American consumer than to advance the welfare of the developing states. ". . . our first duty," the State Department made clear in November 1962, "is to protect the American consumer."[18]

A detailed survey of the specific agreements in which the United States has participated, such as coffee and sugar, confirms that Washington enters such arrangements to fulfill its explicit public goal of serving its own interests. In the case of the 1964 coffee discussions, at which time the Latin American producers hoped for a twenty-cent-a-pound increase that experts estimated would cost American consumers about a billion dollars a year or more, the United States arranged a voting structure which gave it, in effect, a veto. It also left itself the right of withdrawal within ninety days, which would have led to the destruction of the agreement. Coffee prices by 1967 fell to one-quarter less than the average for 1953–62. The United States has consistently nullified the price-increasing effects of commodity agreements, or has opposed them altogether. That it has gained immeasurably thereby is reflected in the sorry economic state of the nations exporting to keep United States industry running and its people, relative to the rest of the world, affluent.[19]

American Tools for Success

The United States vast expansion in its agricultural exports, and the billions of dollars of lost income to the Third World, reveals the success of the brilliant American synthesis of aid, pressure, and exclusion that is the main characteristic of its foreign economic diplomacy.

The United States is the world's leading state trader, even though it has consistently attacked this principle when other industrial nations used it to advance their own neocolonial export positions. Official American agricultural export subsidy programs involved $3 billion annually in 1957 and 1967, with sums approaching that amount in the interim years. Most of these subsidized exports went to developing nations, often, as in the case of India, in return for vital concessions that aided America's industry, just as agricultural exports aided its big commercial farmers.

Given United States exclusion of many cheaper, freely exportable goods and commodities, and its opposition to higher prices for Third World exports, one can only regard the foreign aid program as a subsidy to American farmers and industry rather than as a gesture of concern for the world's poor. Between 1948 and 1958 ships sailing under the American flag carried 57 percent of the foreign aid despatched from the United States, and Americans owned many of the other vessels flying foreign flags. The United States required aid recipients to spend 68 percent of the aid program expenditures during that period in the United States; American-controlled Middle Eastern oil absorbing part of the remainder. By 1965 over one-third of United States exports to developing countries, which now absorbed nearly one-third of American exports, were directly financed on a tied basis. There were few humanitarian reasons for exporting vast amounts of cotton abroad under these programs, and in fact cheaper cotton was usually available to developing nations from other Third World countries. In reality, the American program cut into intra-Third World trade on behalf of a standing United States policy to maintain a "fair historical share" of the world cotton market for the United States, a figure somewhere around five million bales a year and in no sense a standard of equity.[20]

The aid programs have generated vast quantities of counterpart funds in local currencies, amounting to nearly $2 billion by June 1965, as a result of the obligation of recipient nations to deposit the proceeds of the sales of American aid in jointly controlled accounts. Though not convertible to dollars, these funds have deprived recipient nations of dollar incomes that would have otherwise been available in cases of outright American grants of aid.

American expenses in counterpart countries, ranging from embassy overhead to C.I.A. activities, are limited by convention, but this is optional and the United States can use nearly half of the counterpart resources. In India, which has accounted for half the counterpart funds, United States-controlled rupees were equivalent to more than one-half the money in circulation, and America's ability to dislocate India's economy is now openly acknowledged and discussed. Possible economic warfare aside, counterpart funds not only reflect the United States search for agricultural markets but the desire, as Draper Committee experts recommended in 1959, ". . . to encourage through a form of subsidy without actual cost to the US taxpayer, desirable US industrial investment in selected areas and fields. . . ."[21]

Public Law 480 in 1954 already partially embodied such sophistication. It authorized the United States to use counterpart funds to stockpile raw materials, and the Government acquired $295 million worth of such commodities by September 1956. By 1964 it had used some $1.7 billion in counterpart funds to build military bases and housing, as loans to American businesses, to find new agricultural markets, and similar functions. Despite the rhetorical conservative business complaints about "give-aways," foreign aid essentially has been a means of subsidizing American interests while extending American power in the world economy. "I wish," President Kennedy reminded them in September 1963, "American businessmen who keep talking against the program would realize how significant it has been in assisting them to get into markets where they would have no entry and no experience and which has traditionally been European. . . . Last year 11 percent of our exports were financed under our aid program. And the importance of this aid to our exports is increasing as our developing assistance is increasing, now almost entirely tied to American purchases."[22]

The Loan Syndrome

The Marshall Plan consisted essentially of outright grants to industrialized and potentially rich European nations because it was a program to save Western capitalism, an objective so fundamental in importance to the United States that $13 billion appeared a small price to pay for the survival of world capitalism. The impoverished Third World receives tied American loans, not grants, because this is a major means to extend capitalism and economic control into that sphere. In brief, loans have become a species of imperialism—in many nations more complex and subtle but no less thorough.

By March 1957, when the President's Fairless Committee on foreign aid reported, most American foreign economic planners were inclined to shift more emphatically to a policy of harder loans, repayable in dollars. At the same time, the United States had to solve its growing and persistent balance of payments problem, and in late 1959 it even more firmly tied loans to the required export of American goods as a precondition. In principle, during these years and thereafter, the United States opposed European tied loans, ostensibly because Europe was not faced with a balance of payments problem. If the Latin American nations complained that as a result of such strings associated with the Alliance for Progress loans the United States agencies only forced them to purchase goods far above the cost of European or Japanese equivalents, they were told, as Lincoln Gordon phrased it in March 1966, that the "struggle for freedom in Vietnam" required the practice.[23]

Until the Kennedy Administration, most United States International Cooperation Administration or Development Loan Fund loans were repayable in local funds rather than dollars, and assistance was geared more to contingent grants than loans. After 1961, when Washington created the Agency for International Development, it made development loans repayable in dollars, and by 1965 70 percent of United States development aid was in the form of loans. During this period Congress raised minimum loan rates from three-quarters of 1 percent to 2 and one-half percent, while the Export-Import Bank and World Bank were averaging 5 and one-half percent. As a result, whereas in 1955 debt servicing in the form of interest and repayments offset 8 percent of external assistance to developing countries, by 1964 it had reached 30 percent. In terms of debt servicing as a percentage of income of the recipient nations from foreign exports, the increase was from 3.7 percent in 1956 to 9.1 percent in 1963, with the possibility of more than doubling by 1975. For Latin America the problem is even more grave, as its debt servicing increased from 7.7 percent of its export income in 1957 to 17 percent in 1967. By 1967 servicing external public debt absorbed three-quarters of the gross capital inflow into Latin America, causing a near impasse in regional development via foreign aid. In short, servicing aid was beginning to wipe out the advantages of loans to the developing nations, so that in 1964, for example, the Export-Import Bank received $100 million more from Latin America than it lent to it. Indeed, Export-Import loans result in a net outflow of resources from all its borrowers after about eight years. Since it is the plan of A.I.D. to harden its loan terms, despite the fact that there has already been a rescheduling of the payments of a number of hard-pressed nations, the end result will aggravate the economic position of the developing states.

Then why does the United States loan funds to poor nations that in the long run will lose thereby? First, most of the loans go to build an internal infrastructure which is a vital prerequisite to the development of resources and direct United States private investments. Then there is the fact that to repay loans in dollars requires the borrowing nations to export goods capable of earning them, which is to say, raw materials of every sort. Development in this form increases the Third World's dependence on Western capitalist nations, so that loans become integrating and binding liens. And lastly, as A.I.D. itself explains it,

> Our foreign economic assistance program as a whole has had by-products of substantial benefit to the U.S. economy. For example, Food for Peace has helped us manage our agricultural surpluses while making its important contribution to

development. A.I.D. development loan dollars, now spent in large preponderance in the U.S., contribute substantially to employment in our export industries, and have created important footholds for future U.S. export markets after U.S. assistance is phased out. (Indeed, in considering projects for development financing, A.I.D. now also takes into account any special potential for future trading relationships between the U.S. and recipient countries.)[24]

United States Investment and Trade

The true extent of American investments and control in the world economy is too complex a topic for precise description, for the quality of the data is such that only rough estimates reveal the broad configurations of the vital problem. The known values of United States investments abroad hardly expose the true worth and profitability of American-controlled industries. Using foreign corporate intermediaries, and acquiring local firms via outright purchase (833 in 1965–66 alone), makes the gathering of accurate data all the more difficult. The extensive use of tax havens and false reports on overseas profits and holdings pose yet other problems. Less than one-quarter of the total funds available for all United States investments abroad in 1957 were based on exported dollars; reinvested profits, local borrowing, and depreciation provided the larger bulk. Therefore the investment of American corporate funds abroad carries with it a vast power of internal expansion and multiplication that exceeds known appraisals. The Department of Commerce readily admits that it bases official data on book values rather than true market worth and replacement costs, which Emilio G. Collado of Standard Oil of New Jersey has suggested are at least double the book assessments. By any criterion, what we call United States investment abroad is much more foreign resources mobilized in American hands, generating its own capital in a manner that pyramids the American penetration of the world economy. Whatever else they may be, profits on such investments are not primarily the reward for the transfer of American capital abroad.

With these statistical limitations in mind, direct United States private investments abroad had a book value of $7.5 billion in 1929, and in 1950 were still only $11.8 billion. By 1966 those investments were about five times greater, or $54.6 billion, with an additional $32 billion in other forms of private holdings. Manufacturing investments accounted for $22 billion of this sum, and were preponderately located in Canada and West Europe. Canada and Latin America absorbed the large bulk of the $4.1 billion in mining and smelting, while substantial portions of the $16.3 billion in petroleum were found everywhere, most of all, of course, in the Middle East.[25]

Translated into different terms, indicating economic power and not depending on artificially deflated investment data, United States firms controlled the better part of the world's oil industry. In Germany in 1964, foreign corporations, among whom American companies predominated, owned 90 percent of the petroleum industry, 40 percent of the food, drink, and tobacco industries, and 23 percent each in the automobile and electronics industries. In France, where United States firms accounted for over one-half of the foreign investments, by 1962 eighteen of the one hundred largest French corporations were foreign owned, giving them a powerful position in the leading sector of the economy. And by 1967 American firms in Italy represented at least six percent of all corporate investments there, with especially strong positions in the oil and electronics industries. In 1957 such American-owned firms everywhere in the world supplied 27 percent of the United States imports, with the concentration being much higher in petroleum, minerals, and agricultural commodities. They accounted for one-third of Latin American exports to the world during 1967. Their function, therefore, was not merely to produce vast profits but to supply essential American needs. Their relative economic power in the countries in which they operated was, at the very least, great.

Despite Washington's more recent desire to balance its payments via lower dollar exports, it has directed this restrictive program mainly to West Europe rather than the developing world, for investments in the latter are critical to sustain and expand the output of raw materials the United States requires. In fact, the recent leveling off in European economic growth, devaluation and further threats of it, have all contributed to a slight reduction in American investments in Europe since 1966 in any case. But these are transitory fluctuations which in no way diminish the powerful position of American industry and finance abroad, and its profound involvement in the fate of the world economy and everything that affects it.

American foreign investments are unusually parasitic, not merely in the manner in which they use a minimum amount of dollars to mobilize maximum foreign resources, but also because of the United States crucial position in the world raw-materials price structure both as consumer and exporter. This is especially true in the developing regions, where extractive industries and cheap labor result in the smallest permanent foreign contributions to national wealth. In Latin America in 1957, for example, 36 percent of United States manufacturing investments, as opposed to 56 percent in Europe and 78 percent in Canada, went for plant and equipment. And wages as a percentage of operating costs in United States manufacturing investments are far lower in Third World nations than Europe or Canada.[26]

Actual annual profits on United States investments abroad are difficult to calculate, not only for the same complexities mentioned in estimating the true worth of investments, but for larger structural reasons as well. For example, the United

States industry's predominance in Middle Eastern oil sources also makes possible its control over Western European oil refining and sales, and opens new means of earning profits on Third World investments. Suffice it to say, the official figures are quite minimal, as the Commerce Department readily admits. Even so, between 1950 and 1966 the annual yields in all United States direct private investments abroad were at least a low of 11.5 percent in 1966 to at least a high of 19 percent in 1951. However, this lumps Europe and the Third World, manufacturing and oil, together in a totally meaningless fashion, for American profits in the Third World are generally greater. United States petroleum earnings on investment in Latin America between 1951–55, *after* local taxes, were an annual average of 25.6 percent, and 20.5 percent in 1956–58. Petroleum quite consistently has returned the largest annual returns on any form of investment, and this has meant resources depletion and a vast loss to the Third World, if not in the past under feudal and reactionary regimes then most assuredly in the future.

Several other indices are perhaps more to the point in suggesting the relative significance of world trade and the developing nations to United States prosperity. The sales of the foreign affiliates of American manufacturing firms in the first half of this decade grew much faster than those of their domestic components, and one can haphazardly measure this comparatively high profit and sales in a manner that reveals the dimensions of American interests. International oil firms, of course, are well known for their dependence on world sources. But in 1961 the foreign subsidiaries of the Aluminum Corporation of America generated 65 percent of its net income, 80 percent of Yale & Towne's net earnings, 78 percent of Colgate-Palmolive's profits, 35 percent of Corn Products' sales, and 48 percent of Pfizer's total volume. Forty-four of the one hundred top United States industrial corporations in the same year were no less dependent on their overseas branches for sales and profits, and during the mid-1960's only 70 United States firms accounted for nearly one-half of the American investments in developing countries.

Another approach is to estimate the ability of direct United States investments to originate profits. For example, between 1950–60 the $30.5 billion in earnings in all areas was almost equal to the accumulated book value of all American direct investments in the world, though in Latin America profits were higher than the total investments there. During 1961–66 earnings in the entire world added another $28.8 billion, making the return on investment in only seventeen years considerably larger than its total book value since the post-1890 period. This profit was again more pronounced from Latin America and the Middle East.[27] Even assuming that the book value represents the net capital outflow from the United States, which is certainly not the case, profits on foreign investments have been extremely large during the postwar period of Third World revolution and hunger.

Seen in this light, United States foreign aid has been a tool for penetrating and making lucrative the Third World in particular and the entire nonsocialist world in general. The small price for saving European capitalism made possible later vast dividends, the expansion of American capitalism, and ever greater power and profits. It is this broader capability eventually to expand and realize the ultimate potential of a region that we must recall when short-term cost accounting and a narrow view make costly American commitments to a nation or region inexplicable. Quite apart from profits on investments, during 1950–60 the United States allocated $27.3 billion in nonmilitary grants, including the agricultural disposal program. During that same period it exported $166 billion in goods on a commercial basis, and imported materials essential to the very operation of the American economy.[28] It is these vast flows of goods, profits, and wealth that set the fundamental context for the implementation and direction of United States foreign policy in the world.

The United States and the Price of Stability

Under conditions in which the United States has been the major beneficiary of a world economy geared to serve it, the continued, invariable American opposition to basic innovations and reforms in world economic relations is entirely predictable. Not merely resistance to stabilizing commodity and price agreements, or non-tied grants and loans, but to every imperatively needed structural change has characterized United States policy toward the Third World. In short, the United States is today the bastion of the *ancien regime,* of stagnation and continued poverty for the Third World.

There was never any secret in the decade and a half after the war that the basic foreign economic policy of the United States posited that "The U.S. is convinced that private ownership and operation of industrial and extractive enterprises contribute more effectively than public ownership and operation to the general improvement of the economy of a country. . . . It is therefore a basic policy of the I.C.A. to employ U.S. assistance to aid-receiving countries in such a way as will encourage the development of the private sectors of their economies."[29] Both personally and publicly, American leaders felt, as Douglas Dillon "most emphatically" phrased it, ". . . aid to a foreign country is no substitute for the adoption of sound economic policies on the part of that country."[30]

Invariably, this meant opening the doors of developing nations to American investments and the support for pliable *comprador* elements wherever they could be found, in the belief, to cite Secretary of Treasury George M. Humphrey, that "There are hundreds of energetic people in the world who are better equipped than governments ever can be to risk huge sums in search, exploration, and development wherever the laws of the country will give them half a chance."[31]

The implications of such a policy were great, requiring intervention to save American investors and friendly conservative governments, and above all the maximization of raw materials production for export to the fluctuating world market. "Our purpose," Percy W. Bidwell wrote in his studies for the Council on Foreign Relations, "should be to encourage the expansion of low-cost production and to make sure that neither nationalistic policies nor Communist influences deny American industries access on reasonable terms to the basic materials necessary to the continued growth of the American economy."[32] Hence nationalism and modest but genuine reform were quite as great an enemy as bolshevism. This meant that via diplomatic pressures and contingent loans and aid the United States engaged in what Eugene Black has called "development diplomacy" throughout the world, a strategy that attempts to show that "The desire for autarky will not be tempered until there is more awareness of how, by underemphasizing exports, the leaders of these nations are prolonging the poverty of their people."[33] That fluctuating raw materials prices and immense foreign profits were crucial handicaps to the problems of development was of no consequence, since the primary objective of the United States was to serve its own interests.

The advancement of American capitalism and an open field for development in the Third World were the guiding principles of American diplomacy, both on the part of government and business leaders. This has required, in turn, specific opposition to every measure likely to alleviate Third World misery at the expense of the industrial nations. Land reform, especially in Latin American nations, is now regarded essentially as a problem of increasing productivity rather than broadening tenure or redistributing land. The United States has opposed measures to stop the so-called "brain drain" which now brings 30,000 professionals and technically trained migrants to the United States each year (not counting nonreturning foreign students who are educated here), about one-third of them from Third World countries. In fact this also represents the annual transfer of hundreds of millions of dollars of educational investment to the United States.

Global efforts to revise the terms of trade go beyond commodity agreements, but the United States opposed such reforms at the United Nations Conference on Trade and Development at Geneva in March 1964, where the American delegation found itself in the uncomfortable position of disputing nearly all Third World proposals. At the Delhi session in March 1968 the United States position was seemingly more liberal, but geared to the unattainable precondition that France and England give up their preferential agreements with former colonies, even though the United States has its own with the Philippines and Puerto Rico. Significantly, the United States has also consistently opposed the creation of a meaningful Latin American "free trade" area. In principle, if such blocs lower costs of production, conserve scarce exchange, or improve the terms of trade, they can develop into effective means for development. In fact, both the Common Market and European special agreements in Africa and Asia have filled the United States with profound reservations concerning all new exclusionary trade blocs, for in practice they have tended to close off United States trade. Indeed, a Latin American trade zone would not make sense if it qualified as a true free-trade bloc into which the United States could export and invest without planned economic development, and since only restrictionism in one form or another will improve Latin economic conditions the United States has ranged itself against meaningful Latin American economic integration.[34]

The numerous American interventions to protect its investors throughout the world, and the United States ability to use foreign aid and loans as a lever to extract required conformity and concessions, have been more significant as a measure of its practice. The instances of this are too plentiful to detail here, but the remarkable relationship between American complaints on this score and the demise of objectionable local political leaders deserves more than passing reference.

When, in May 1963, the Indonesian Government insisted on taking over its oil industry, the American threat to discontinue foreign aid forced Sukarno to accept an agreement that left the American firms with effective control of the industry. Later that year similiar scenarios were repeated in Peru and Argentina, also involving oil, as the United States linked the future of aid and the Alliance for Progress directly to its private investments. At the end of the year President Goulart of Brazil attacked the Alliance as a means of United States hemispheric domination and a poor substitute for a Latin trade bloc intended to obtain higher earnings for exports. Some months later, in April 1964, President Johnson sent his "warmest wishes" to the leaders of the coup who had overthrown Goulart, and at the end of 1964 Hanna Mining and Bethlehem Steel obtained vast iron ore concessions in Brazil.[35]

The relationship between the objectives of foreign economic policy and direct political and military intervention therefore has been a continuous and intimate one—indeed, very often identical. If historians have glossed over this dimension, in part because of lack of access to data but also due to a fashionable theory of economic nondeterminism, it is sufficient to point out that the critical premises and world view of America's leaders make this element in American foreign policy since the Second World War the one that needs far greater appreciation and inquiry. During the early stage of the Suez Crisis, in August 1956, John Foster Dulles, in a meeting with the presidents of American oil firms, made explicit the premise that, as a Socony Vacuum executive recorded his words, ". . . the United States would not acquiesce in the rights of nationalization that would affect any other facilities in our own economic interests. . . . He commented that international law recognizes the right to nationalize if adequate compensation is paid, but he admits that actually adequate compensation is never really paid and nationalization, in effect, thereby becomes confiscation. . . . the United States felt it was O.K. to nationalize only if assets were not impressed with international interest. What he meant by international interest was where a foreign government had made promises of fixed duration in the form of concessions or contracts, upon which other nations would rely on fixing their courses of action and their own economies. . . . Therefore . . . nationalization of this kind of an asset impressed with international interest goes far beyond composition of shareholders alone, and should call for international intervention."[36]

This formula, as vague as it is concerning the unknown value of minerals in the ground or the ideological basis of necessary economic planning, was broad enough to lead to United States belligerence toward the Cuban revolution from its very first days and to a whole host of other crises involving American property abroad. Succinctly, it aligned the United States against any radical changes in the internal affairs of national economies in which it had some interest, and required interventionism as a consistent response. Where United States troops and threats of violence did not accompany the intervention, various economic pressures, embargoes, and the like accomplished the task. Hoping to stem the tide of Third World economic conflicts with American objectives, by October 1964 the United States had signed investment guaranty treaties against convertibility changes with sixty-six countries and against expropriation with sixty-four. Congress, with enthusiasm that often exceeded even that of the Executive branch, has repeatedly declared its support for private investment as the best means for economic development in the Third World, and in summer 1964 surpassed itself in unsuccessfully attempting to transfer to American courts the right to judge the legality of foreign expropriations.[37] The effort was superfluous, for in the preceding decades and later years the United States Government made it abundantly clear that its function in the world was to protect and advance American economic power in the control of the world economy.

That function, in the final analysis, required a monumental inconsistency between America's practice and what it advocated as acceptable conduct for the rest of the world. Such a role demanded, as well, that the United States take a stand against every political and economic movement in the world designed not even to revolutionize national societies but merely to shift the distribution of the world's wealth away from American borders. In effect, this conservative policy compelled the United States to confront the competitive European nations as well as Left nationalist and revolutionary governments, and its choice of responses depends on the stakes and countervailing power involved.

A Theory of United States Global Role

In their brilliant essay on the political economy of nineteenth century British imperialism, John Gallagher and Ronald Robinson have described a process that parallels the nature of United States expansion after 1945:

> Imperialism, perhaps, may be defined as a sufficient political function of this process of integrating new regions into the expanding economy; its character is largely decided by the various and changing relationships between the political and economic elements of expansion in any particular region and time. Two qualifications must be made. First, imperialism may

be only indirectly connected with economic integration in that it sometimes extends beyond areas of economic development, but acts for their strategic protection. Secondly, although imperialism is a function of economic expansion, it is not a necessary function. Whether imperialist phenomena show themselves or not, is determined not only by the factors of economic expansion, but equally by the political and social organization of the regions brought into the orbit of the expansive society, and also by the world situation in general.

It is only when the politics of these new regions fail to provide satisfactory conditions for commercial or strategic integration and when their relative weakness allows, that power is used imperialistically to adjust those conditions. Economic expansion, it is true, will tend to flow into the regions of maximum opportunity, but maximum opportunity depends as much upon political considerations of security as upon questions of profit. Consequently, in any particular region, if economic opportunity seems large but political security small, then full absorption into the extending economy tends to be frustrated until power is exerted upon the state in question. Conversely, in proportion as satisfactory political frameworks are brought into being in this way, the frequency of imperialist intervention lessens and imperialist control is correspondingly relaxed. It may be suggested that this willingness to limit the use of paramount power to establishing security for trade is the distinctive feature of the British imperialism of free trade in the nineteenth century, in contrast to the mercantilist use of power to obtain commercial supremacy and monopoly through political possession.[38]

In today's context, we should regard United States political and strategic intervention as a rational overhead charge for its present and future freedom to act and expand. One must also point out that however high that cost may appear today, in the history of United States diplomacy specific American economic interests in a country or region have often defined the national interest on the assumption that the nation can identify its welfare with the profits of some of its citizens— whether in oil, cotton, or bananas. The costs to the state as a whole are less consequential than the desires and profits of specific class strata and their need to operate everywhere in a manner that, collectively, brings vast prosperity to the United States and its rulers.

Today it is a fact that capitalism in one country is a long-term physical and economic impossibility without a drastic shift in the distribution of the world's income. Isolated, the United States would face those domestic backlogged economic and social problems and weaknesses it has deferred confronting for over two decades, and its disappearing strength in a global context would soon open the door to the internal dynamics which might jeopardize the very existence of liberal corporate capitalism at home. It is logical to regard Vietnam, therefore, as the inevitable cost of maintaining United States imperial power, a step toward saving the future in something akin to its present form by revealing to others in the Third World what they too may encounter should they also seek to control their own development. That Vietnam itself has relatively little of value to the United States is all the more significant as an example of America's determination to hold the line as a matter of principle against revolutionary movements. What is at stake, according to the "domino" theory with which Washington accurately perceives the world, is the control of Vietnam's neighbors, Southeast Asia and, ultimately, Latin America.

The contemporary world crisis, in brief, is a by-product of United States response to Third World change and its own definitions of what it must do to preserve and expand its vital national interests. At the present moment, the larger relationships in the Third World economy benefit the United States, and it is this type of structure America is struggling to preserve. Moreover, the United States requires the option to expand to regions it has not yet penetrated, a fact which not only brings it into conflict with Third World revolutions but also with an increasingly powerful European capitalism. Where neocolonial economic penetration via loans, aid, or attacks on balanced economic development or diversification in the Third World are not sufficient to maintain stability, direct interventions to save local *compradors* and oligarchies often follow. Frequently such encroachments succeed, as in Greece and the Dominican Republic, but at times, such as Vietnam, it is the very process of intervention itself that creates its own defeat by deranging an already moribund society, polarizing options, and compelling men to choose—and to resist. Even the returns to the United States on partial successes have warranted the entire undertaking in the form not just of high profit ratios and exports, but in the existence of a vast world economic sector which supplies the disproportionately important materials without which American prosperity within its present social framework would eventually dry up.

The existing global political and economic structure, with all its stagnation and misery, has not only brought the United States billions but has made possible, above all, a vast power that requires total world economic integration not on the basis of equality but of domination. And to preserve this form of world is vital to the men who run the American economy and politics at the highest levels. If some of them now reluctantly believe that Vietnam was not the place to make the final defense against tides of unpredictable revolutionary change, they all concede that they must do it somewhere, and the logic of their larger view makes their shift on Vietnam a matter of expediency or tactics rather than of principle. All the various American leaders believe in global stability which they are committed to defend against revolution that may threaten the existing distribution of economic power in the world.

When the day arrives that the United States cannot create or threaten further Vietnams, the issue at stake will be no less than the power of the United States in the world. At that point, both the United States and the rest of the world will undergo a period of profound crises and trauma, at home as well as abroad, as the allocation of the earth's economic power is increasingly removed from American control. *If,* in the process of defending their prerogatives, the leaders of the United States during those trying years do not destroy the globe, piecemeal as in Vietnam or in a war with China or Russia, we shall be on the verge of a fundamentally new era for the United States and mankind. The elimination of that American hegemony is the essential precondition for the emergence of a nation and a world in which mass hunger, suppression, and war are no longer the inevitable and continuous characteristics of modern civilization.

★
★ ★
★ 4 ★
★ ★
★

THE UNITED STATES

IN VIETNAM, 1944–66:

ORIGINS AND OBJECTIVES

THE INTERVENTION of the United States in Vietnam is the most important single embodiment of the power and purposes of American foreign policy since the Second World War, and no other crisis reveals so much of the basic motivating forces and objectives—and weaknesses—of American global politics. A theory of the origins and meaning of the war also discloses the origins of an American malaise that is global in its reaches, impinging on this nation's conduct everywhere. To understand Vietnam is also to comprehend not just the present purposes of American action but also to anticipate its thrust and direction in the future.

Vietnam illustrates, as well, the nature of the American internal political process and decision-making structure when it exceeds the views of a major sector of the people, for no other event of our generation has turned such a large proportion of the nation against its government's policy or so profoundly alienated its youth. And at no time has the government conceded so little to democratic sentiment, pursuing as it has a policy of escalation that reveals that its policy is formulated not with an eye to democratic sanctions and compromises but rather the attainment of specific interests and goals scarcely shared by the vast majority of the nation.

The inability of the United States to apply its vast material and economic power to compensate for the ideological and human superiority of revolutionary and guerrilla movements throughout the world has been the core of its frustration in Vietnam. From a purely economic viewpoint, the United States cannot maintain its existing vital dominating relationship to much of the Third World unless it can keep the poor nations from moving too far toward the Left and the Cuban or Vietnamese path. A widespread leftward movement would critically affect its supply of raw materials and have profound long-term repercussions. It is the American view of the need for relative internal stability within the poorer nations that has resulted in a long list of United States interventions since 1946 into the affairs of numerous nations, from Greece to Guatemala, of which Vietnam is only the consummate example—but in principle no different than numerous others. The accuracy of the "domino" theory, with its projection of the eventual loss of whole regions to American direction and access, explains the direct continuity between the larger United States global strategy and Vietnam.

Yet, ironically, while the United States struggles in Vietnam and the Third World to retain its own mastery, or to continue that once held by the former colonial powers, it simultaneously weakens itself in its deepening economic conflict with Europe, revealing the limits of America's power to attain its ambition to define the preconditions and direction of global economic and political developments. Vietnam is essentially an American intervention against a nationalist, revolutionary agrarian movement which embodies social elements in incipient and similar forms of development in numerous other Third World nations. It is in no sense a civil war, with the United States supporting one local faction against another, but an effort to preserve a mode of traditional colonialism via a minute, historically opportunistic *comprador* class in Saigon. For the United States to fail in Vietnam would be to make the point that even the massive intervention of the most powerful nation in the history of the world was insufficient to stem profoundly popular social and national revolutions throughout the world. Such a revelation of American weaknesses would be tantamount to a demotion of the United States from its present role as the world's dominant superpower.

Given the scope of United States ambitions in relation to the Third World, and the sheer physical limits on the successful implementation of such a policy, Vietnam also reveals the passivity of the American Military Establishment in formulating global objectives that are intrinsically economic and geopolitical in character. Civilians, above all, have calculated the applications of American power in Vietnam and their strategies have prompted each military escalation according to their definitions of American interests. Even in conditions of consistent military impotence and defeat, Vietnam has fully revealed the tractable character of the American military when confronted with civilian authority, and their continuous willingness to obey civilian orders loyally.

It is in this broader framework of the roots of United States foreign policy since 1945 that we must comprehend the history and causes of the war in Vietnam and relate it to the larger setting of the goals of America's leaders and the function of United States power in the modern world.

★

Throughout the Second World War the leaders of the United States scarcely considered the future of Indo-China, but during 1943 President Roosevelt suggested that Indo-China become a four-power trusteeship after the war, proposing that the eventual independence of the Indo-Chinese might follow in twenty to thirty years. No one speculated whether such a policy would require American troops, but it was clear that the removal of French power was motivated by a desire to penalize French collaboration with Germany and Japan, or De Gaulle's annoying independence, rather than a belief in the intrinsic value of freedom for the Vietnamese. Yet what was critical in the very first American position was that ultimate independence would not be something that the Vietnamese might take themselves, but a blessing the other Great Powers might grant at their own convenience. Implicit in this attitude was the seed of opposition to the independence movement that already existed in Vietnam.[1] Indeed, all factors being equal, the policy toward European colonialism would depend on the extent to which the involved European nations accepted American objectives elsewhere, but also the nature of the local opposition. If the Left led the independence movements, as in the Philippines, Korea, or Indo-China, then the United States sustained collaborationist alternatives, if possible, or endorsed colonialism.

Although Roosevelt at Yalta repeated his desire for a trusteeship, during March 1945 he considered the possibility of French restoration in return for their pledge eventually to grant independence. But by May 1945 there was no written, affirmative directive on United States political policy in Indo-China. The gap was in part due to the low priority assigned the issue, but also reflected growing apprehension as to what the future of those countries as independent states might hold.[2]

At the Potsdam Conference of July 1945, and again in the General Order Number 1 the United States unilaterally issued several weeks later, the remaining equivocation on Indo-China was resolved by authorizing the British takeover of the nation south of the 16th parallel and Chinese occupation north of it, and this definitely meant the restoration of the French whom the British had loyally supported since 1943. One cannot exaggerate the importance of these steps, since it made the United States responsible for the French return at a time when Washington might have dictated the independence of that nation. By this time everyone understood what the British were going to do.

Given the alternative, United States support for the return of France to Indo-China was logical as a means of stopping the triumph of the Left, a question not only in that nation but throughout the Far East. Moreover, by mid-August French officials were hinting that they would grant the United States and England equal economic access to Indo-China. Both in action and thought the United States Government now chose the reimposition of French colonialism. At the end of August De Gaulle was in Washington, and the President now told the French leader that the United States favored the return of France to Indo-China. The decision would shape the course of world history for decades.[3]

The O.S.S. worked with the Vietminh, a coalition of Left and moderate Resistance forces led by Ho Chi Minh, during the final months of the war to the extent of giving them petty quantities of arms in exchange for information and assistance with downed pilots, and they soon came to know Ho and many of the Vietminh leaders. Despite the almost paranoid belief of the French representatives that the O.S.S. was working against France, the O.S.S. only helped consolidate Washington's support for the French.[4] They and other American military men who arrived in Hanoi during the first heady days of freedom were unanimous in believing that Ho ". . . is an old revolutionist . . . a product of Moscow, a communist."[5] The O.S.S. understood the nationalist ingredient in the Vietnamese revolution, but they emphasized the Communist in their reports to Washington.[6]

During September the first British troops began arriving in the Indo-Chinese zone which the Americans assigned them

and imposed their control over half of a nation largely Vietminh controlled with the backing of the vast majority of the
people. The British arranged to bring in French troops as
quickly as they might be found, and employed Japanese
troops in the Saigon region and elsewhere. ". . . [On] the
23rd September," the British commander later reported to his
superiors, "Major-General Gracey had agreed with the French
that they should carry out a *coup d'état;* and with his permis-
sion, they seized control of the administration of Saigon and
the French Government was installed."[7] The State Department's representative who visited Hanoi the following month
found the references of the Vietnamese to classic democratic
rhetoric mawkish, and "Perhaps naively, and without consideration of the conflicting postwar interests of the 'Big' nations
themselves, the new government believed that by complying
with the conditions of the wartime United Nations conferences
it could invoke the benefits of these conferences in favor of its
own independence."[8] From this viewpoint, even in 1945 the
United States regarded Indo-China almost exclusively as the
object of Great Power diplomacy and conflict. By the end of
the Second World War the Vietnamese were already in violent
conflict not only with the representatives of France, but also
England and the United States, a conflict in which they could
turn the wartime political rhetoric against the governments
that had casually written it. But, at no time did the desires of
the Vietnamese themselves assume a role in the shaping of
United States policy.

1946–49: United States Inaction and the Genesis of a Firm Policy

It is sufficient to note that by early 1947 the American doctrine of containment of communism obligated the United
States to think also of the dangers Ho Chi Minh and the Viet-

minh posed, a movement the United States analyzed as a monolith directed from Moscow. It is also essential to remain aware of the fact that the global perspective of the United States between 1946 and 1949 stressed the decisive importance of Europe to the future of world power. When the United States looked at Indo-China they saw France, and through it Europe, and a weak France would open the door to communism in Europe. But for no other reason, this meant a tolerant attitude toward the bloody French policy in Vietnam, one the French insisted was essential to the maintenance of their empire and prosperity, and the political stability of the nation. Washington saw Vietnamese nationalism as a tool of the Communists.

In February 1947 Secretary of State George C. Marshall publicly declared he wished "a pacific basis of adjustment of the difficulties could be found," but he offered no means toward that end.[9] Given the greater fear of communism, such mild American criticisms of French policy as were made should not obscure the much more significant backing of basic French policy in Washington. By early 1949 Washington had shown its full commitment to the larger assumptions of French policy and goals, and when Bao Dai, the former head of the Japanese puppet regime, signed an agreement with the French in March 1949 to bring Vietnam into the French Union, the State Department welcomed the new arrangement as ". . . the basis for the progressive realization of the legitimate aspirations of the Vietnamese people."[10] Such words belied the reality, for the course of affairs in Asia worried Washington anew.

The catalysis for a reconsideration of the significance of Vietnam to the United States was the final victory of the Communists in China. In July 1949 the State Department authorized a secret reassessment of American policy in Asia in light of the defeat of the Kuomintang, and appointed Ambassador-at-Large Philip Jessup chairman of a special committee. On July 18th Dean Acheson sent Jessup a memo defining the limits of the inquiry: "You will please take as your assumption that it is a fundamental decision of American policy that the United States does not intend to permit further extension of Communist domination on the continent of Asia or in the southeast Asia area. . . ."[11] At the end of 1949 the State Department was still convinced the future of world power remained in Europe, but, as was soon to become evident, this involved the necessity of French victory in Vietnam. Most significant about the Jessup Committee's views was the belief, as one State Department official put it, "In respect to Southeast Asia we are on the fringes of crisis," one that, he added, might involve all of Asia following China.[12] It appears to have been the consensus that Bao Dai, despite American wishes for his success, had only the slimmest chance for creating an effective alternative to Ho in Vietnam. The Committee compared French prospects to those of Chiang Kai-shek two years earlier, and since they acknowledged that the Vietminh captured most of their arms from the French, the likelihood of stemming the tide seemed dismal.

There were two dimensions to the Vietnam problem from the United States viewpoint at the end of 1949. First, it was determined to stop the sweep of revolution in Asia along the fringes of China, and by that time Vietnam was the most likely outlet for any United States action. Second, it was believed that small colonial wars were draining France, and therefore Europe, of its power. Yet a Western victory had to terminate these struggles in order to fortify Europe, the central arena of the Cold War. "I found all the French troops of any quality were out in Indo-China," Marshall complained to the Jessup Committee, ". . . and the one place they were not was in Western Europe. So it left us in an extraordinarily weak position there. . . ."[13] Massive American intervention in Vietnam was now inevitable.

1950–53: America Escalates the War in Indo-China

The significance of the struggle in Vietnam for the United States always remained a global one, and for this reason Vietnam after 1950 became the most sustained and important single issue confronting Washington. The imminent crisis in Asia that the Jessup Committee had predicted was one John Foster Dulles, even then one of the key architects of United States diplomacy, also anticipated. Dulles, however, thought it a mistake to place the main emphasis on American policy in Europe, and he, like everyone else in Washington, was not in the least impressed by the future of the Associated States of Vietnam, Laos, and Cambodia which the United States recognized on February 7, 1950, with a flurry of noble references to independence and democracy. A "series of disasters can be prevented," Dulles advised in May 1950, "if at some doubtful point we quickly take a dramatic and strong stand that shows our confidence and resolution. Probably this series of disasters cannot be prevented in any other way." It would be necessary, he believed, even to "risk war."[14]

The official position of the Truman Administration at this time was to insist on regarding Vietnam as essentially an extension of a European affair. As Charles E. Bohlen of the State Department explained it in a top secret briefing in April:

> As to Indo-China, if the current war there continues for two or three years, we will get very little of sound military development in France. On the other hand, if we can help France to get out of the existing stalemate in Indo-China, France can do something effective in Western Europe. The

need in Indo-China is to develop a local force which can maintain order in the areas theoretically pacified. . . .

It is important, in order to maintain the French effort in Indo-China, that any assistance we give be presented as defense of the French Union, as the French soldiers there would have little enthusiasm for sacrificing themselves to fight for a completely free Indo-China in which France would have no part.[15]

Suffice it to say, the French were hard-pressed economically, and they needed United States aid on any terms, and in May 1950 direct United States economic aid was begun to Cambodia, Laos, and Vietnam. Immediately after the Korean affair Truman pledged greater support to the French and the Bao Dai regime.[16]

During mid-October 1950, shortly after some serious military reverses, Jules Moch, the French Minister of National Defense, arrived in Washington to attempt to obtain even greater United States military aid. By this time, despite earlier reticence, the French had come to realize that the key to their colonial war was in Washington.

The aggregate military aid the United States contributed to the French effort in Vietnam is a difficult matter of bookkeeping, but total direct military aid to France in 1950–1953 was $2,956,000,000, plus $684 million in 1954. United States claims suggest that $1.54 billion in aid was given to Indo-China before the Geneva Accords, and in fact Truman's statement in January 1953 that the United States paid for as much as half of the war seems accurate enough, and aid rose every year to 1954.[17] The manner in which this aid was disbursed is more significant.

The United States paid but did not appreciate French political direction, though no serious political pressure was put on the French until 1954. Dulles, for one, was aware of Bao

Dai's political unreliability and inability to create an alternative to the Vietminh, and he regretted it. "It seems," he wrote a friend in October 1950, "as is often the case, it is necessary as a practical matter to choose the lesser of two evils because the theoretically ideal solution is not possible for many reasons —the French policy being only one. As a matter of fact, the French policy has considerably changed for the better. . . ."[18] It was Dulles, in the middle of 1951, who discovered in Bao Dai's former premier under the Japanese, Ngo Dinh Diem, the political solution for Indo-China. At the end of 1950 he was willing to content himself with the belief that the expansion of communism in Asia must be stopped. The French might serve that role, at least for a time.

In developing a rationale for United States aid three major arguments were advanced, only one of which was later to disappear as a major source of the conduct of United States policy in Vietnam. First of all, the United States wished to bring France back to Europe via victory in Vietnam: "The sooner they bring it to a successful conclusion," Henry Cabot Lodge explained in early 1951, "the better it would be for NATO because they could move their forces here and increase their building of their army in Europe. . . ."[19] The French insistence until 1954 of blocking German rearmament and the European Defense Community until they could exist on the continent with military superiority over the Germans, a condition that was impossible until the war in Vietnam ended, gave this even more persuasive consideration special urgency. From this viewpoint, Vietnam was the indirect key to Germany. In the meantime, as Ambassador to France David Bruce explained it, "I think it would be a disaster if the French did not continue their effort in Indo-China."[20]

Victory rather than a political settlement was necessary because of the two other basic and more permanent factors in guiding United States policy. The United States was always convinced that the "domino" theory would operate should Vietnam remain with the Vietnamese people. "There is no question," Bruce told a Senate committee, "that if Indo-China went, the fall of Burma and the fall of Thailand would be absolutely inevitable. No one can convince me, for what it is worth, that Malay wouldn't follow shortly thereafter, and India . . . would . . . also find the Communists making infiltrations. . . ."[21] The political character of the regime in Vietnam was less consequential than the larger United States design for the area, and the seeds of future United States policy were already forecast when Bruce suggested that ". . . the Indo-Chinese—and I am speaking now of the . . . anti-Communist group—will have to show a far greater ability to live up to the obligations of nationhood before it will be safe to withdraw, whether it be French Union forces or any other foreign forces, from that country."[22] If the French left, someone would have to replace them.

Should Vietnam, and through it Asia, fall to the Vietminh, then the last major American fear would be realized. ". . . [Of] all the prizes Russia could bite off in the east," Bruce also suggested, "the possession of Indo-China would be the most valuable and in the long run would be the most crucial one from the standpoint of the west in the east. That would be true not because of the flow of rice, rubber, and so forth . . . but because it is the only place where any war is now being conducted to try to suppress the overtaking of the whole area of southeast Asia by the Communists."[23] Eisenhower and Nixon put this assumption rather differently, with greater emphasis on the value of raw materials, but it has been a constant basis of United States policy in Vietnam since 1951. "Why is the United States spending hundreds of millions of dollars supporting the forces of the French Union in the fight against communism?" Vice President Richard Nixon asked in December 1953. "If Indo-China falls, Thailand is put in an almost impossible position. The same is true of Malaya with its rubber and tin. The same is true of Indonesia. If this whole part of Southeast Asia goes under Communist domination or Communist influence, Japan, who trades and must trade with this area in order to exist, must inevitably be oriented towards the Communist regime."[24] "The loss of all Vietnam," Eisenhower wrote in his memoir, "together with Laos on the west and Cambodia on the southwest, would have meant the surrender to Communist enslavement of millions. On the material side, it would have spelled the loss of valuable deposits of tin and prodigious supplies of rubber and rice. It would have meant that Thailand, enjoying buffer territory between itself and Red China, would be exposed on its entire eastern border to infiltration or attack. And if Indo-China fell, not only Thailand but Burma and Malaya would be threatened, with added risks to East Pakistan and South Asia as well as to all Indonesia."[25]

Given this larger American conception of the importance of the Vietnam war to its self-interest, which impelled the United States to support it financially, the future of the war no longer depended largely on whether the French would fight or meet the demands of the Vietnamese for independence. Already in early 1952 Secretary of State Dean Acheson told Foreign Minister Anthony Eden, as recorded in the latter's memoir, ". . . of the United States' determination to do everything possible to strengthen the French hand in Indo-China. On the wider question of the possibility of a Chinese invasion, the United States Government considered that it would be disastrous to the position of the Western powers if South-East Asia were lost without a struggle."[26] If Acheson promised prudence by merely greatly increasing arms aid to the French, he also talked of blockading China. The war, even by 1952, was being internationalized with America assuming ever greater initiative for its control. When Eisenhower came to the Presidency in January 1953, Acheson presented Vietnam to him as "an urgent matter on which the new administration must be prepared to act."[27] Given Dulles' experience and views on the question, Acheson's words were not to be wasted.

By spring 1953 the United States Government was fully aware of the largely tangential role of the French in its larger global strategy, and it was widely believed in Congress that if the French pulled out the United States would not permit Vietnam to fall. The United States was increasingly irritated with the French direction of affairs. The economic aid sent to Vietnam resulted merely in the creation of a speculative market for piastres and dollars which helped the local *compradors* enrich themselves while debilitating the economy. "Failure of important elements of the local population to give a full measure of support to the war effort remained one of the chief negative factors," the State Department confided to Eisenhower.[28] ". . . [It] was almost impossible," Eisenhower later wrote, "to make the average Vietnamese peasant realize that the French, under whose rule his people had lived for some eighty years, were really fighting in the cause of freedom, while the Vietminh, people of their own ethnic origins, were fighting on the side of slavery."[29] Bao Dai, whom the United States had always mistrusted, now disturbed the Americans because, as Eisenhower recalls, he ". . . chose to spend the bulk of his time in the spas of Europe. . . ."[30]

The French, for their part, were now divided on the proper response the massive American intervention into the war demanded. But during July 1953 Bidault and Dulles conferred and Dulles promised all the French desired, also admonishing them not to seek a negotiated end to the war. In September the United States agreed to give the French a special grant of $385 million to implement the Navarre Plan, a scheme to build French and puppet troops to a level permitting them to destroy the regular Vietminh forces by the end of 1955. By this time the essential strategy of the war supplanted a strict concern for bringing France back to NATO, and the Americans increasingly determined to make Vietnam a testing ground for a larger global strategy of which the French would be the instrument. Critical to that strategy was military victory.

The difficulty for the United States undertaking was that, as General LeClerc had suggested several years earlier, there was ". . . no military solution for Vietnam."[31] The major foreign policy crisis of late 1953 and early 1954, involving Dulles' confusing "massive retaliation" speech of January 12, 1954, was the first immediate consequence of the failure of the Navarre Plan and the obvious French march toward defeat. The vital problem for the United States was how it might apply its vast military power in a manner that avoided a land war in the jungles, one which Dulles always opposed in Asia and which the Americans too might lose. At the end of December 1953 Dulles publicly alluded to the possibility that in the event of a Chinese invasion of Vietnam the Americans might respond by attacking China, which several weeks later was expressed again in the ambiguous threat of the American need ". . . to be willing and able to respond vigorously at places and with means of its own choosing."[32] Every critical assumption on which the United States based its foreign and military policy they were now testing in Vietnam.

1954: The Geneva Conference

Given the larger regional, even global, context of the question of Vietnam for the United States, a peaceful settlement would have undermined the vital premise of Washington since 1947 that one could not negotiate with communism but only contain it via military expenditures, bases, and power. In February 1954, as Eden records, ". . . our Ambassador was told at the State Department that the United States Government were perturbed by the fact that the French were aiming not to win the war, but to get into a position from which they could negotiate."³³ The United States was hostile to any political concessions and to an end to the war. To the French, many of whom still wished to fight, the essential question was whether the United States Government would share the burden of combat as well as the expense. The French would make this the test of their ultimate policy.

At the end of March the French sought to obtain some hint of the direction of United States commitments, and posed the hypothetical question of what United States policy would be if the Chinese used their aircraft to attack French positions. Dulles refused to answer the question, but he did state that if the United States entered the war with its own manpower, it would demand a much greater share of the political and executive direction of the future of the area.³⁴

It is probable the United States Government in the weeks before Geneva had yet to define a firm policy for itself save on one issue: the desire not to lose any part of Vietnam by negotiations and to treat the existing military realities of the war as the final determining reality. Eden's memory was correct when he noted that in April the Undersecretary of State, Walter Bedell Smith, informed the English Government ". . . that the United States had carefully studied the partition solution, but had decided that it would only be a temporary palliative and would lead to Communist domination of South-East Asia."³⁵

During these tense days words from the United States were extremely belligerent, but it ultimately avoided equivalent actions, and laid the basis for later intervention. On March 29th Dulles excoriated Ho and the Vietminh and all who ". . . whip up the spirit of nationalism so that it becomes violent." He again reiterated the critical value of Vietnam as a source of raw materials and its strategic value in the area, and now blamed China for the continuation of the war. After detailing the alleged history of broken Soviet treaties, Dulles made it clear that the United States would go to Geneva so that ". . . any Indo-China discussion will serve to bring the Chinese Communists to see the danger of their apparent design for the conquest of Southeast Asia, so that they will cease and desist."[36] Vice President Richard Nixon on April 16th was rather more blunt in a press conference: Geneva would become an instrument of action and not a forum for a settlement. ". . . [The] United States must go to Geneva and take a positive stand for united action by the free world. Otherwise it will have to take on the problem alone and try to sell it to others. . . . This country is the only nation politically strong enough at home to take a position that will save Asia. . . . Negotiations with the Communists to divide the territory would result in Communist domination of a vital new area."[37]

The fact the United States focused on Chinese "responsibility" for a war of liberation from the French that began in 1945, years before the Chinese Communists were near the south, was not only poor propaganda but totally irrelevant as a basis of military action. There was at this time no effective means for United States entry into the war, and such power as the Americans had would not be useful in what ultimately had to be a land war if they could hope for victory. War hawks aside, the Pentagon maintained a realistic assessment of the problem of joining the war at this time from a weak and fast-crumbling base, and for this reason the United States never implemented the much publicized schemes for entering the war via air power. The United States Government was, willy-nilly, grasping at a new course, one that had no place for Geneva and its very partial recognition of realities in Vietnam.

On April 4th Eisenhower proposed to Churchill that the three major NATO allies, the Associated States, the ANZUS countries, Thailand, and the Philippines form a coalition to take a firm stand on Indo-China, by using naval and air power against the Chinese coast and intervening in Vietnam itself. The British were instantly cool to the amorphous notion, and they were to insist that first the diplomats do their best at Geneva to save the French from their disastrous position. Only the idea of a regional military alliance appealed to them.[38] Despite much scurrying and bluster, Dulles could not keep the British and French from going to Geneva open to offers, concessions, and a *détente*.

On May 7th, the day before the Geneva Conference turned to the question of Vietnam, Laos, and Cambodia, Dien Bien Phu fell to the victorious Vietnamese. Psychologically, though not militarily, the United States saw this as a major defeat in Vietnam. Militarily, about three-quarters of Vietnam belonged to the Vietnamese and imminent French defeat promised to liberate the remainder. That same evening Dulles went on the radio to denounce Ho as a "Communist . . . trained in Moscow" who would ". . . deprive Japan of important foreign markets and sources of food and raw materials."[39] Vietnam, Dulles went on, could not fall "into hostile hands," for then "the Communists could move into all of Southeast Asia."[40] Nevertheless, "The present conditions there do not provide a suitable basis for the United States to participate with its armed forces," and so the hard-pressed French might wish an armistice. "But we would be gravely concerned if an armistice or cease-fire were reached at Geneva which would provide a road to a Communist takeover and further aggression."[41]

The United States position meant an explicit denial of the logic of the military realities, for negotiations to deprive the Vietminh of all of their triumphs was, in effect, a request for surrender. Even before the Conference turned to the subject, the United States rejected—on behalf of a larger global view which was to make Vietnam bear the brunt of future interventions—the implications of a negotiated settlement.

The Geneva Agreement

Others have authoritatively documented the United States role during the Geneva Conference discussion of May 8–July 21— the indecision, vacillation, and American refusal to acknowledge the military and political realities of the time. The British, for their part, hoped for partition, the Russians and the Chinese for peace—increasingly at any price—and the Vietnamese for Vietnam and the political rewards of their near-military triumph over a powerful nation. The American position, as the *New York Times* described it during these weeks, was ". . . driving the U.S. deeper into diplomatic isolation on Southeast Asian questions," and "Though the U.S. opposes . . . these agreements, there appears to be little the U.S. can do to stop them."[42]

To the Vietnamese delegation led by Pham Van Dong, the question was how to avoid being deprived of the political concomitant of their military triumph, and they were the first to quickly insist on national elections in Vietnam at an early date—elections they were certain to win. As the Conference proceeded, and the Russians and then the Chinese applied pressure for Vietnamese concessions on a wide spectrum of issues —the most important being the provisional zonal demarcation along the 17th parallel—the importance of this election provision became ever greater to the Vietminh.

To both the Vietnamese and the United States partition as a permanent solution was out of the question, and Pham Van Dong made it perfectly explicit that zonal regroupments were only a temporary measure to enforce a cease-fire. Had the Vietminh felt it was to be permanent they unquestionably would not have agreed to the Accords. When Mendès-France conceded a specific date for an election, the world correctly interpreted it as a major concession to Vietnamese independence. By the end of June, the Vietnamese were ready to grant much in the hope that an election would be held. During these very same days, Eden finally convinced the United States that a partition of Vietnam was all they might hope for, and on June 29th Eden and Dulles issued a statement which agreed to respect an armistice that "Does not contain political provisions which would risk loss of the retained area to Communist control."[43] Since that loss was now inevitable, it ambiguously suggested that the United States might look askance at elections, or the entire Accord itself. When the time came formally to join the other nations at Geneva in endorsing the Conference resolutions, the United States would not consent to do so.

The final terms of the Accords are too well known for more than a contextual résumé here. The "Agreement on Cessation of Hostilities" that the French and Vietnamese signed on July 20th explicitly described as "provisional" the demarcation line at the 17th parallel. Until general elections, the Vietnamese and French respectively were to exercise civil authority above and below the demarcation line, and it was France alone that had responsibility for assuring conformity to its terms on a political level. Militarily, an International Control Commission was to enforce the terms. Arms could not be increased beyond existing levels. Article 18 stipulated ". . . the establishment of new military bases is prohibited throughout Viet-Nam territory," and Article 19 that "the two parties shall ensure that the zones assigned to them do not adhere to any military alliance," which meant that Vietnam could not join the Southeast Asia Treaty Organization the United States was beginning to organize.[44] The Final Declaration issued on July 21st "takes note" of these military agreements, and ". . . that the essential purpose of the agreement relating to Viet-Nam is to settle military questions with a view to ending hostilities and that the military demarcation line is provisional and

should not in any way be interpreted as constituting a political
or territorial boundary."[45] Vietnam was one nation in this
view, and at no place did the documents refer to "North" or
"South." To achieve political unity, ". . . general elections
shall be held in July 1956, under the supervision of an international control commission . . . ," and "Consultations will
be held on this subject between the competent representative
authorities of the two zones from 20 July 1955 onwards."[46]

To the United States it was inconceivable that the French
and their Vietnamese allies could implement the election pro-
viso without risk of total disaster. It is worth quoting Eisenhower's two references to this assumption in his memoir: "It
was generally conceded that had an election been held, Ho
Chi Minh would have been elected Premier."[47] "I have never
talked or corresponded with a person knowledgeable in Indo-
Chinese affairs who did not agree that had elections been held
as of the time of the fighting, possibly 80 percent of the population would have voted for the Communist Ho Chi Minh as
their leader rather than Chief of State Bao Dai."[48]

The United States therefore could not join in voting for the
Conference resolution of July 21st, and a careful reading of
the two United States statements issued unilaterally the same
day indicates it is quite erroneous to suggest that the United
States was ready to recognize the outcome of a Conference
and negotiated settlement which it had bitterly opposed at
every phase. Eisenhower's statement begrudgingly welcomed
an end to the fighting, but then made it quite plain that ". . .
the United States has not itself been a party to or bound by the
decisions taken by the Conference, but it is our hope that it
will lead to the establishment of peace consistent with the
rights and needs of the countries concerned. The agreement
contains features which we do not like, but a great deal depends on how they work in practice."[49] The ". . . United

States will not use force to disturb the settlement. We also say that any renewal of Communist aggression would be viewed by us as a matter of grave concern."[50] Walter Bedell Smith's formal statement at Geneva made the same points, but explicitly refused to endorse the 13th article of the Agreement requiring consultation by the members of the Conference to consider questions submitted to them by the I.C.C., ". . . to ensure that the agreements on the cessation of hostilities in Cambodia, Laos and Viet-Nam are respected."[51]

The Aftermath of Geneva:
The U.S. Entrenchment, 1955–59

The United States attached such grave reservations because it never had any intention of implementing the Geneva Accords, and this was clear from all the initial public statements. The *Wall Street Journal* was entirely correct when on July 23rd it reported that "The U.S. is in no hurry for elections to unite Viet Nam; we fear Red leader Ho Chi Minh would win. So Dulles plans first to make the southern half a showplace—with American aid."[52]

While various United States missions began moving into the area Diem controlled, Dulles addressed himself to the task of creating a SEATO organization which, as Eisenhower informed the Senate, was ". . . for defense against both open armed attack and internal subversion."[53] To Dulles from this time onward, the SEATO treaty would cover Vietnam, Cambodia, and Laos, even though they failed to sign the Treaty and in fact the Geneva Agreement forbade them to do so. Article IV of the SEATO treaty extended beyond the signatories and threatened intervention by the organization in case of aggression "against any State or territory" in the region, or if there was a threat to the "political independence . . . of any other

State or territory. . . ."⁵⁴ Under such an umbrella the United States might rationalize almost any intervention for any reason.

The general pattern of United States economic and military aid to the Diem regime between 1955 and 1959, which totaled $2.92 billion in that period, indicates the magnitude of the American commitment, $1.71 billion of which was advanced under military programs, including well over a half-billion dollars before the final Geneva-scheduled election date.

That elections would never be held was a foregone conclusion, despite the efforts of the North Vietnamese, who on the first of January 1955 reminded the French of their obligations to see the provision respected. Given the internecine condition of the local opposition and its own vast strength among the people, the Democratic Republic of Vietnam had every reason to comply with the Geneva provisos on elections. During February 1955 Hanoi proposed establishing normal relations between the two zones preparatory to elections, and Pham Van Dong in April issued a joint statement with Nehru urging steps to hold elections to reunify the country. By this time Diem was busy repressing and liquidating internal opposition of every political hue, and when it received no positive answer to its June 6th pleas for elections, the D.R.V. again formally reiterated its opposition to the partition of one nation and the need to hold elections on schedule. During June the world turned its attention to Diem's and Dulles' response prior to the July 20th deadline for consultations. Diem's response was painfully vague, and the first real statement came from Dulles on June 28th when he stated neither the United States nor the regime in the south had signed the Agreement at Geneva or was bound to it, a point that Washington often repeated and which was, in the case of the south, patently false. Nevertheless, Dulles admitted that in principle the United States favored ". . . the unification of countries which have a historic unity," the myth of two Vietnams and two nations not yet being a part of the American case. "The Communists have never yet won any free election. I don't think they ever will. Therefore, we are not afraid at all of elections, provided they are held under conditions of genuine freedom which the Geneva armistice agreement calls for."[55] But the United States, it was clear from this statement, was not bound to call for the implementation of the agreement via prior consultations which Diem and Washington had refused until that time, nor did Dulles say he would now urge Diem to take such a course.

Diem at the end of April 1955 announced he would hold a "national referendum" in the south to convoke a new national assembly, and on July 16th he categorically rejected truly national elections under the terms of Geneva until ". . . proof is . . . given that they put the superior interests of the national community above those of Communism. . . ."[56] "We certainly agree," Dulles stated shortly thereafter, "that conditions are not ripe for free elections."[57] The response of the D.R.V. was as it had always been: Geneva obligated the Conference members to assume responsibility for its implementation, including consultations preparatory to actual elections, and in this regard Diem was by no means the responsible party. But the English favored partition, and the French were not about to thwart the United States Government. The fraudulent referendum of October 23rd which Diem organized in the south gave Diem 98 percent of the votes for the Presidency of the new "Government of Vietnam." Three days later Washington replied to the news by recognizing the legitimacy of the regime.[58]

In reality, using a regime almost entirely financed with its funds, and incapable of surviving without its aid, the United States partitioned Vietnam.

To the D.R.V., the United States and the Diem Administrations' refusal to conform to the Geneva Accords was a question for the members of the Geneva Conference and the I.C.C. to confront, and while it had often made such demands—during June and again November 1955, and directly to Diem on July 19th—in September and again on November 17, 1955, Pham and Ho publicly elaborated their ideas on the structure of an election along entirely democratic lines. All citizens above eighteen could vote and all above twenty-one could run for office. They proposed free campaigning in both zones and secret and direct balloting. The I.C.C. could supervise. On February 25, 1956, Ho again reiterated this position.

On February 14, 1956, Pham Van Dong directed a letter to the Geneva co-chairmen pointing to the repression in the south, its de facto involvement in an alliance with the United States, and the French responsibility for rectifying the situation. He now proposed that the Geneva Conference reconvene to settle peacefully the problem of Vietnam. The British refused, and again on April 6th the Diem government announced that "it does not consider itself bound by their provisions."[59] On May 8th the Geneva co-chairmen sent to the north and south, as well as to the French, a demand to open consultations on elections with a view to unifying the country under the Geneva Accords. Three days later the D.R.V. expressed readiness to begin direct talks in early June at a time set by the Diem authorities. Diem refused. The D.R.V. continued to demand consultations to organize elections, submitting notes to this effect to the Geneva co-chairmen and the Diem government in June and July 1957, March and December 1958, July 1959 and July 1960, and later, for arms reduction, resumption of trade, and other steps necessary to end the artificial partition of Vietnam. These proposals failed, for neither Diem nor the United States could survive their successful implementation.[60]

Washington's policy during this period was clear and publicly stated. On June 1, 1956, after visiting Diem with Dulles the prior March, Walter S. Robertson, Assistant Secretary of State, attacked the Geneva Accords, which ". . . partitioned [Vietnam] by fiat of the great powers against the will of the Vietnamese people." He lauded Diem's rigged "free election of last March" and stated the American determination "To support a friendly non-Communist government in Viet-Nam and to help it diminish and eventually eradicate Communist subversion and influence. . . . Our efforts are directed first of all toward helping to sustain the internal security forces consisting of a regular army of about 150,000 men, a mobile civil guard of some 45,000, and local defense units. . . . We are also helping to organize, train, and equip the Vietnamese police force."[61] Such policies were, of course, in violation of the Geneva Accords forbidding military expansion.

The term "eradicate" was an apt description of the policy which the United States urged upon the more-than-willing Diem, who persecuted former Vietminh supporters, dissident religious sects, and others. An estimated 40,000 Vietnamese were in jail for political reasons by the end of 1958, almost four times that number by the end of 1961. Such policies were possible because the United States financed over 70 percent of Diem's budget, and the main United States emphasis was on the use of force and repression. There were an estimated minimum of 16,600 political liquidations between 1955–59, perhaps much higher. Suffice it to say, every objective observer has accepted *Life* magazine's description in May 1957 as a fair estimate:

Behind a facade of photographs, flags and slogans there is a grim structure of decrees, "re-education centers," secret police. Presidential "Ordinance No. 6" signed and issued by Diem in January, 1956, provides that "individuals considered dangerous to national defense and common security may be

confined on executive order" in a "concentration camp." . . .
Only known or suspected Communists . . . are supposed to
be arrested and "re-educated" under these decrees. But many
non-Communists have also been detained . . . The whole
machinery of security has been used to discourage active opposition of any kind from any source.[62]

The International Control Commission's teams complained
of these violations in the south, and in the north they claimed
that the only significant group to have its civil liberties in-
fringed was the Catholic minority, approximately one-tenth of
the nation. The cooperation of the D.R.V. with the I.C.C. was
a critical index of its intentions, and an example of its naïve
persistence in the belief Geneva had not in reality deprived
them of its hard-fought victory. The vast military build-up in
the south made real cooperation with the I.C.C. impossible,
and its complaints, especially in regard to the airfields and re-
prisals against civilians, were very common. In certain cases
the Diem regime permitted I.C.C. teams to move in the south,
but it imposed time limits, especially after 1959. Although
there is no precise way of making a count of what figures both
Diem and the United States were attempting to hide, by July
1958 the D.R.V.'s estimate that Diem had 450,000 men under
arms was probably correct in light of Robertson's earlier estimate of United States plans and the $1.7 billion in military ex-
penditures for Diem through 1959.[63]

Although the large bulk of American aid to Diem went to
military purposes, the section devoted to economic ends further
rooted an entirely dependent regime to the United States. That
economic aid was a total disaster, exacerbated a moribund
economy, ripped apart the urban society already tottering
from the first decade of war, and enriched Diem, his family,
and clique. Yet certain germane aspects of the condition of the
southern economy are essential to understand the next phase
of the revolution in Vietnam and further American interven-

tion, a revolution the Americans had frozen for a time but could not stop.

The Vietminh controlled well over one-half the land south of the 18th parallel prior to the Geneva Conference, and since 1941 they had managed to introduce far-reaching land reform into an agrarian economy of grossly inequitable holdings. When Diem took over this area, with the advice of United States experts he introduced a "land reform" program which in fact was a regressive "modernization" of the concentrated land control system that had already been wiped out in many regions. Saigon reduced rents by as much as 50 percent from pre-Vietminh times, but in fact it represented a reimposition of tolls that had ceased to exist in wide areas. In cases of outright expropriation, landlords received compensation for property that they had already lost. In brief, the Diem regime's return to power meant a reimposition of a new form of the prewar 1940 land distribution system in which 72 percent of the population owned 13 percent of the land and two-thirds of the agricultural population consisted of tenants ground down by high rents and exorbitant interest rates. For this reason, it was the landlords rather than the peasantry who supported "agrarian reform."

Various plans for resettling peasants in former Vietminh strongholds, abortive steps which finally culminated in the strategic hamlet movement of 1962, simply helped to keep the countryside in seething discontent. These *agrovilles* uprooted traditional villages and became famous as sources of discontent against the regime, one which was ripping apart the existing social structure. In brief, Diem and the United States never established control over the larger part of south Vietnam and the Vietminh's impregnable peasant base, and given the decentralization and the corruption of Diem's authority, there was no effective basis for their doing so. The repression Diem exercised only rekindled resistance.[64]

In the cities the dislocations in the urban population, constantly augmented by a flow of Catholic refugees from the north, led to a conservative estimate in 1956 of 413,000 unemployed out of the Saigon population of two million. The $1.2 billion in nonmilitary aid given to the Diem regime during 1955–59 went in large part to pay for its vast import deficit which permitted vast quantities of American-made luxury goods to be brought into the country's inflationary economy for the use of the new *comprador* class and Diem's bureaucracy.

The United States endorsed and encouraged the military build-up and repression, but it did not like the strange mélange of mandarin anti-capitalism and Catholic feudalism which Diem jumbled together in his philosophy of personalism. Diem was a puppet, but a not perfectly tractable one. The United States did not appreciate the high margin of personal graft, nor did it like Diem's hostility toward accelerated economic development, nor his belief in state-owned companies. Ngo Dinh Nhu, his brother, regarded economic aid as a cynical means of dumping American surpluses, and the United States had to fight, though successfully, for the relaxation of restrictions on foreign investments and protection against the threat of nationalization. Ultimately Diem was content to complain and to hoard aid funds for purposes the United States thought dubious.

The U.S. thought of Vietnam as a capitalist state in Southeast Asia. This course condemned it to failure, but in April 1959, when Eisenhower publicly discussed Vietnam, ". . . a country divided into two parts," and not two distinct nations, he stressed Vietnam's need to develop economically, and the way ". . . to get the necessary capital is through private investments from the outside and through government loans," the latter, insofar as the United States was concerned, going to local capitalists.[65]

1959–64: The Resistance Is Rekindled

Every credible historical account of the origins of the armed struggle south of the 17th parallel treats it as if it were on a continuum from the war with the French of 1945–54, and as the effect rather than the cause of the Diem regime's frightful repression and accumulated internal economic and social problems. The resistance to Diem's officials had begun among the peasantry in a spontaneous manner, by growing numbers of persecuted political figures of every persuasion, augmented by Buddhists and Vietminh who returned to the villages to escape, and, like every successful guerrilla movement, it was based on the support of the peasantry for its erratic but ultimately irresistible momentum. On May 6, 1959, Diem passed his famous Law 10/59 which applied the sentence of death to anyone committing murder, destroying to any extent houses, farms, or buildings of any kind, means of transport, and a whole list of similar offenses. "Whoever belongs to an organization designed to help to prepare or perpetuate crimes . . . or takes pledges to do so, will be subject to the sentences provided. . . ."[66] The regime especially persecuted former members of the Vietminh, but all opposition came under the sweeping authority of Diem's new law, and the number of political prisoners between 1958 and the end of 1961 quadrupled. The resistance that spread did not originate from the north, and former Vietminh members joined the spontaneous local resistance groups well before the D.R.V. indicated any support for them. Only in 1960 did significant fighting spread throughout the country.

At the end of 1960 the United States claimed to have only 773 troops stationed there. By December 1965 there were at least fourteen major United States airbases in Vietnam, 166,000 troops, and the manpower was to more than double over the following year.[67] This build-up violated the Geneva

Accords, but that infraction is a fine point in light of the fact that the United States always had utter contempt for that agreement. In reality, the United States was now compelled to save what little it controlled of the south of Vietnam from the inevitable failure of its own policies.

It is largely pointless to deal with the subsequent events in the same detail, for they were merely a logical extension of the global policies of the United States before 1960. One has merely to juxtapose the newspaper accounts in the United States press against the official rationalizations cited in Washington to realize how very distant from the truth Washington was willing to wander to seek justification for a barbaric war against a small nation quite unprecedented in the history of modern times. To understand this war one must always place it in its contextual relationship and recall that the issues in Vietnam were really those of the future of United States power not only in Southeast Asia but throughout the entire developing world. In Vietnam the United States Government has vainly attempted to make vast power relevant to international social and political realities that had bypassed the functional conservatism of a nation seeking to save an old order with liberal rhetoric and, above all, with every form of military power available in its nonnuclear arsenal.

By 1960 it was apparent that Diem would not survive very long, a point that an abortive palace revolt of his own paratroop battalions emphasized on November 11th. When Kennedy came to office amidst great debates over military credibility and the need to build a limited-war capability, Vietnam inevitably became the central challenge to the intellectual strategists he brought to Washington. In May 1961, Kennedy and Dean Rusk denounced what they called D.R.V. responsibility for the growth of guerrilla activity in the south, a decision Rusk claimed the Communist Party of the D.R.V. made in May 1959 and reaffirmed in September of the following year.

This tendentious reasoning, of course, ignored the fact that the prior September, Pham Van Dong again urged negotiations on the basis of reciprocal concessions in order to achieve unity without recourse to "war and force."[68] By the fall two missions headed by Eugene Staley and the leading limited-war theorist, General Maxwell Taylor, went to Vietnam to study the situation. On October 18th Diem declared a state of emergency, and on November 16th Kennedy pledged a sharp increase in aid to the regime, which newspapers predicted would also involve large United States troop increases. During November the *Wall Street Journal,* for example, admitted that aid would be going to a regime characterized by "corruption and favoritism," and described the "authoritarian nature of the country" which allowed the National Liberation Front, formed at the end of December 1960, to build up a mass base among ". . . the farmers who welcome an alternative to corrupt and ineffective appointees of the regime."[69]

The United States Government could hardly admit that the problem in southern Vietnam was the people's revolt against the corruption of an oppressive regime that survived only with American guns and dollars, and not very well at that, and so it was necessary, while once again violating the Geneva Accords, to build up the myth of intervention from the D.R.V. At this time the United States Government effected a curious shift in its attitude toward the Geneva Accords, from denouncing or ignoring it to insisting that it bound the other side and, implicitly, that the United States had endorsed it. When asked about how a vast increase in United States military aid affected the agreement, Washington from this time on insisted, in Rusk's words, that ". . . the primary question about the Geneva Accords is not how those Accords relate to, say, our military assistance program to south Vietnam. They relate to the specific, persistent, substantial, and openly proclaimed violations of those accords by the north Vietnamese. . . . The first question is, what does the north do about those accords?"[70] "If the North Vietnamese bring themselves into full compliance with the Geneva Accords," Rusk stated on December 8th as he released the so-called White Paper, "there will be no problem on the part of South Vietnam or any one supporting South Vietnam."[71] Only the prior month Ho publicly called for the peaceful reunification of the country via the terms of Geneva.[72] Not surprisingly, Rusk never referred to the question of elections.

The United States White Paper of December 1961 was inept, and an excellent source of information for disproving nearly all the American claims of the time. It consisted of a mélange of data, case histories, and quotes from D.R.V. statements, most obviously out of context. As for China or Russia supplying the N.L.F. with arms, the White Paper admitted "The weapons of the VC are largely French- or U.S.-made, or handmade on primitive forges in the jungle."[73] Evidence ranged from South Vietnamese interrogation records to reproductions of human anatomy from a Chinese text book to photos of medical equipment made in China and the cover of a private diary. The White Paper exhibited no military equipment and the long extracts from various D.R.V. congresses and publications revealed merely that the D.R.V. was officially committed to ". . . struggle tenaciously for the implementation of the Geneva agreements" and "peaceful reunification of the fatherland."[74] The State Department's incompetent case was less consequential than the renewed and frank exposition of the "domino" theory: if all of Vietnam chose the leadership of Ho and his party, the rest of Asia would "fall." Above all, as the American press acknowledged, if the United States did not intervene the shabby Diem regime would collapse without anything acceptable replacing it.[75]

During early 1962 the United States announced and began the Staley Plan—Operation Sunrise—for razing existing villages and regrouping entire populations against their will; and in February created a formal command in Vietnam. Officially, to meet I.C.C. complaints, the United States reported 685 American soldiers were in Vietnam, but in fact reporters described the truth more accurately, and Washington intensified a long pattern of official deception of the American public. Yet the United States position was unenviable, for on February 27th Diem's own planes bombed his palace. This phase of the story need not be surveyed here—more pliable and equally corrupt men were to replace Diem. As one American officer in April 1962 reported of growing N.L.F. power, "When I arrived last September, the Vietcong were rarely encountered in groups exceeding four or five. Now they are frequently met in bands of forty to sixty."[76]

On March 1st, while alleging D.R.V. responsibility for the war, Rusk declared its ". . . all in gross violation of the Geneva Accords." The problem, he argued over the following years, came from the north. As for the D.R.V.'s appeal that the Geneva Conference be reconvened, he suggested "There is no problem in South Vietnam if the other side would stay its hand. . . . I don't at the moment envisage any particular form of discussion. . . ."[77] No later than March, American forces in Vietnam were actively locked in combat.

Despite propaganda of the lowest calibre which the State Department and White House issued, more authoritative statements from various Government agencies indicated reluctance to base planning on the fiction that the D.R.V. started the war in Vietnam. The Senate Committee on Foreign Relations report of January 1963 admitted that the N.L.F., ". . . is equipped largely with primitive, antiquated, and captured weapons."[78] Despite the weakness of the N.L.F. in this regard against a regular army of well over 150,000, plus police, etc., "By 1961 it was apparent that the prospects for a total collapse in south Vietnam had begun to come dangerously close."[79]

American intervention had stayed that event. Speaking to the Senate Armed Services Committee in early March, General David Shoup, Commandant of the Marine Corps, freely admitted there was no correlation between the size of the N.L.F. and the alleged infiltrators from the north: "I don't agree that they come in there in the numbers that are down there. . . ."[80] Not until July 1963 did the United States publicly and unequivocally claim that, for the first time, it had captured N.L.F. arms manufactured in Communist countries after 1954.

By the summer of 1963 it was obvious that the American Government and its ally Diem were headed toward military defeat in Vietnam and new and unprecedented political resistance at home. Diem's oppression of all political elements, his active persecution of the Buddhists, the failure of the strategic hamlet program, the utter incompetence of his drafted troops against far weaker N.L.F. forces the American press described in detail. At the beginning of September Washington was apparently bent on pressuring Diem but preserving him against mounting Buddhist protests, but as Kennedy admitted on September 9th as audible stirrings from senators were heard for the first time, "What I am concerned about is that Americans will get impatient and say, because they don't like events in Southeast Asia or they don't like the Government in Saigon, that we should withdraw."[81] Quite simply, he stated four days later, "If it helps to win the war, we support it. What interferes with the war effort we oppose."[82] The Americans would not sink with Diem.

On October 21st, after some weeks of similar actions on forms of economic aid, the United States Embassy in Saigon announced that it would terminate the pay for Diem's own special political army unless they went into the field. On October 30th this private guard was sent out of Saigon. The next day a military coup brought Diem's long rule to an end.[83]

The United States recognized the new Minh coup on November 4th, amid disturbing reports of continued squabbling within its ranks. On the 8th Rusk confirmed that the mood in Washington was now tending toward winning military victory by rejecting a neutralist solution for Vietnam south of the 17th parallel, linking it to "far-reaching changes in North Vietnam," again insisting that the north was responsible for aggression. "The other side was fully committed—fully committed—in the original Geneva settlement of 1954 to the arrangements which provided for South Vietnam as an independent entity, and we see no reason to modify those in the direction of a larger influence of North Vietnam or Hanoi in South Vietnam."[84] The creation of this deliberate fiction of two Vietnams—North and South—as being the result of the Geneva Accords now indicated that the United States Government would seek military victory.

The new regimes were as unsatisfactory as the old one, and by mid-December the American press reported dissatisfaction in Washington over the dismal drift of the war. In his important dispatches in the *New York Times* at the end of 1963, David Halberstam described the failure of the strategic hamlet program, the corruption of Diem, the paralysis of Minh in these terms: "The outlook is that the situation will deteriorate unless the Government can wrest the initiative from the guerrillas. Unless it can, there appears to be only two likely alternatives. One is a neutralist settlement. The other is the use of United States combat troops to prop up the Government."[85]

The drift toward a neutralist solution at the beginning of 1964 was so great that Washington sought to nip it in the bud. In his New Year's Message to the Minh regime, President Johnson made it clear that ". . . neutralization of South Vietnam would only be another name for a Communist takeover. Peace will return to your country just as soon as the authorities in Hanoi cease and desist from their terrorist aggression."[86] Peace would be acceptable to the Americans after total victory. To alter their losing course, they would escalate.

At the end of January, as the Khanh coup took over, one of the new ruler's grievances against his former allies was that some had surreptitiously used the French Government to seek a neutral political solution. During February, the *New York Times* reported that Washington was planning an attack on the north, with divided counsels on its extent or even its relevance to internal political-economic problems. The United States preferred air bombing and/or a blockade, because as Hanson Baldwin wrote on March 6th, "The waging of guerrilla war by the South Vietnamese in North Vietnam has, in fact, been tried on a small scale, but so far it has been completely ineffective."[87]

On March 15th Johnson again endorsed the "domino" theory and avowed his resolution not to tolerate defeat. On March 26th McNamara in a major address stressed the "great strategic significance" of the issue, and Vietnam as ". . . a major test case of communism's new strategy" of local revolution, one that might extend to all the world unless foiled in Vietnam. Behind the D.R.V., the Secretary of Defense alleged, stood China. The Americans rejected neutralism for Vietnam, reaffirmed aid to the Khanh regime, and darkly hinted at escalation toward the north.[88] During these same days, for the first time in two decades key members of the Senate voiced significant opposition to a major foreign policy. It had become a tradition in the Cold War for Presidents to marshal support from Congress by creating crises, thereby defining the tone of American foreign policy via a sequence of sudden challenges which, at least to some, vindicated their diabolical explanations. A "crisis" was in the making.

All of the dangers of the Vietnamese internal situation persisted throughout spring 1964. On July 24th the *New York Times* reported that Khanh was exerting tremendous pressures on the United States to take the war to the north, even by "liberating" it. During these same days both the French, Soviet, and N.L.F. leaders joined U Thant in a new diplomatic drive to seek an end to the war by negotiations. Washington, for its part, resisted these pacific solutions.

On August 4th Johnson announced that North Vietnamese torpedo boats had wantonly attacked the U.S. destroyer *Maddox* in the Bay of Tonkin and in international waters, and as a result of repeated skirmishes since the 2nd he had ordered the bombardment of North Vietnamese installations supporting the boats. The following day he asked Congress to pass a resolution authorizing him to take all action necessary "to protect our Armed Forces."[89] It was maudlin, fictional, and successful.

It was known—and immediately documented in *Le Monde* —that the United States had been sending espionage missions to the north since 1957—as Baldwin alluded the prior February—and that on July 30th South Vietnamese and United States ships raided and bombarded D.R.V. islands. It was too farfetched that D.R.V. torpedo boats would have searched out on the high seas the ships of the most powerful fleet in the world, without scoring any hits which the United States might show the skeptical world. On August 5th the press asked McNamara for his explanation of the events. "I can't explain them. They were unprovoked. . . . our vessels were clearly in international waters. . . . roughly 60 miles off the North Vietnamese coast." When asked whether reports of South Vietnamese attacks in the area during the prior days were relevant, McNamara demurred! "No, to the best of my knowledge, there were no operations during the period. . . ."[90] In testimony before the Senate during the same days it emerged that United States warships were not sixty miles but three to eleven miles off D.R.V. territory, even though, like many states, the D.R.V. claimed a twelve-mile territorial limit. Over subsequent days more and more information leaked out so that the essential points of the D.R.V. case were confirmed, the long history of raids on the north revealed. By the end of September the entire fantasy was so implausible that the *New York Times* reported that the Defense Department was sending a team to Vietnam to deal with what were euphemistically described as "contradictory reports." They did not subsequently provide further details, for ". . . contributing to the Defense Department's reticence was the secret mission of the two destroyers," a mission the *New York Times* described as espionage of various sorts.[91]

The United States escalated in the hope that it could mobilize a Congress at home and sustain the Khanh regime in Vietnam, which nevertheless fell the following month. During these days the United States Government admitted that the war was now grinding to a total halt as the Vietnamese politicians in the south devoted all their energy to byzantine intrigues. With or without war against the D.R.V., the United States was even further from victory. In assessing the condition in the south a year after the downfall of Diem, the *New York Times* reported from Saigon that three years after the massive increase of the American commitment, and a year after Diem's demise, ". . . the weakness of the Government [has] . . . once again brought the country to the brink of collapse. . . . Once again many American and Vietnamese officials are thinking of new, enlarged commitments—this time to carry the conflict beyond the frontier of South Vietnam."[92]

The Bombing of the D.R.V.

On December 20, 1964, there was yet another coup in Saigon, and during the subsequent weeks the difficulties for the United States resulting from the court maneuvers among generals who refused to fight were compounded by the growing militancy of the Buddhist forces. By January of 1965 the desertion rate within the South Vietnamese Army reached 30 percent among draftees within six weeks of induction, and a very large proportion of the remainder would not fight. It was perfectly apparent that if anyone was to continue the war the United States would have to supply not only money, arms, and 23,000 supporting troops as of the end of 1964, but fight the entire war itself. During January, as well, a Soviet-led effort to end the war through negotiations was gathering momentum, and at the beginning of February Soviet Premier Kosygin, amidst American press reports that Washington in its pessimism was planning decisive new military moves, arrived in Hanoi.

On the morning of February 7th, while Kosygin was in Hanoi, American aircraft bombed the D.R.V., allegedly in response to a N.L.F. mortar attack on the Pleiku base in the south which cost eight American lives. There was nothing unusual in the N.L.F. attack, and every serious observer immediately rejected the official United States explanation, for the Government refused to state that the D.R.V. ordered the Pleiku action, but only claimed the D.R.V. was generally responsible for the war. The United States attack had been prepared in advance, Arthur Krock revealed on February 10th, and the *New York Times* reported that Washington had told several governments of the planned escalation before the 7th. The action was political, not military in purpose, a response to growing dissatisfaction at home and pressures abroad. It was already known that De Gaulle was contemplating a move to reconvene the Geneva Conference—which he attempted on the 10th, after D.R.V. urgings—and during the subsequent weeks, as the United States threatened additional air strikes against the D.R.V., both Kosygin and U Thant vainly attempted to drag the United States Government to the peace table. In response, the Americans now prepared for vast new troop commitments.[93]

On February 26th, the day before the State Department released its second White Paper, Rusk indicated willingness to consider negotiations only if the D.R.V. agreed to stop the war in the south for which he held it responsible. Hence there was no possibility of negotiating on premises which so cynically distorted the facts, and which even Washington understood to be false. ". . . they doubt that Hanoi would be able to call off the guerrilla war," the *New York Times* reported of dominant opinion in Washington barely a week before the Rusk statement.[94] The D.R.V. could not negotiate a war it did not start nor was in a position to end. The United States determined to intervene to save a condition in the south on the verge of utter collapse.

In its own perverse manner, the new White Paper made precisely these points. It ascribed the origins of the war, the "hard core" of the N.L.F., "many" of the weapons to the D.R.V. The actual evidence the Paper gave showed that 179 weapons, or less than 3 percent of the total captured from the N.L.F. in three years, were not definitely French, American, or homemade in origin and modification. Of the small number of actual case studies of captured N.L.F. members offered, the large majority were born south of the 17th parallel and had gone to the north after Geneva, a point that was readily admitted, and which disproved even a case based on the fiction—by now a permanent American premise—that Vietnam was two countries and that those north of an arbitrarily imposed line had no right to define the destiny of one nation.[95] The tendentious case only proved total American responsibility for the vast new increase in the aggression.

Despite the growing pressure for negotiations from many sources, and because of them, by March the United States decided to implement the so-called "McNamara-Bundy Plan" to bring about an "honorable" peace by increasing the war. On March 2nd air strikes against the D.R.V. were initiated once more, but this time they were sustained down to this very day. There were incredulously received rumors of vast increases in troop commitments to as high as 350,000. Washington made an accurate assessment in March 1965 when it realized it could not expect to save Vietnam for its sphere of influence, and that peace was incompatible with its larger global objectives of stopping guerrilla and revolutionary upheavals everywhere in the world. Both McNamara and Taylor during March harked back to the constant theme that the United States was fighting in Vietnam "to halt Communist expansion in Asia."[96] Peace would come, Johnson stated on March 13th, when "Hanoi is prepared or willing or ready to stop doing what it is doing to its neighbors."[97] Twelve days later the President expressed willingness to grant a vast development plan to the region—which soon turned out to be Eugene Black's formula for increasingly specialized raw-materials output for the use of the industrialized world—should the Vietnamese be ready to accept the fiction of D.R.V. responsibility for the war.

It made no difference to the United States Government that on March 22nd the N.L.F., and on April 8th the D.R.V., again called for negotiations on terms which in fact were within the spirit of a Geneva Accords the United States had always rejected. It was less consequential that on April 6th the official Japanese Matsumoto Mission mustered sufficient courage to reject formally the thesis of D.R.V. responsibility for the war in the south and its ability, therefore, to stop the Vietnamese there from resisting the United States and its intriguing puppets. More significant was the fact that, as it announced April 2nd, the Administration had finally decided to send as many as 350,000 troops to Vietnam to attain for the United States what the armies of Diem, Khanh, and others could not—victory. The official position called for "peace," but in his famous Johns Hopkins speech on April 7th Johnson made it clear that "We will not withdraw, either openly or under the cloak of a meaningless agreement." Though he agreed to "unconditional discussions," he made it explicit that these would exclude the N.L.F. and would be with an end to securing ". . . an independent South Vietnam," which is to say permanent partition and a violation of the Geneva Accords.[98] From this time onward the United States persisted in distorting the negotiating position of the D.R.V.'s four-point declaration and effectively ignored the demand of the N.L.F. for "an independent state, democratic, peaceful and neutral." It refused, and has to this day, a voice for the N.L.F. in any negotiations, and insisted that the N.L.F. and D.R.V. had attached certain preconditions to negotiations which in fact did not exist and which on August 3rd the N.L.F. again attempted to clarify—to no avail.

Experience over subsequent years has shown again and again that the words "peace" and "negotiations" from official United States sources were from 1964 onward always preludes to new and more intensive military escalation.[99]

To the United States Government the point of Vietnam is not peace but victory, not just in Vietnam but for a global strategy which it has expressed first of all in Vietnam but at various times on every other continent as well. Johnson's own words in July 1965 stressed this global perspective while attributing the origins of the war to the D.R.V. and, ultimately, China.

> Its goal is to conquer the south, to defeat American power and to extend the Asiatic dominion of Communism.
> And there are great stakes in the balance. . . .
> Our power, therefore, is a very vital shield. If we are driven from the field in Vietnam, then no nation can ever again have the same confidence in American promise or American protection. . . . We did not choose to be the guardians at the gate, but there is no one else.[100]

One does not have to approve of this vision to accept it as an

accurate explanation of why the United States Government is
willing to violate every norm of civilized behavior to sustain
the successive corrupt puppet governments in the south. But
any careful reading of the declarations of Rusk and Mc-
Namara in the months preceding and following this statement
reveals that it was not the Geneva Accords but rather SEATO
and, more critically, the survival of United States power in a
world it can less and less control that has defined the basis of
United States policy in Vietnam. This official policy, as Rusk
expounded it again in March 1966, is that Vietnam is "the
testing ground" for wars of liberation that, if successful in one
place, can spread throughout the world.[101] When, as in January 1966, Undersecretary of State George Ball explained Vietnam ". . . is part of a continuing struggle to prevent the
Communists from upsetting the fragile balance of power
through force or the threat of force," in effect he meant the
ability of the United States to contain revolutionary nationalist movements, Communist and noncommunist alike, unwilling to accept United States hegemony and dedicated to
writing their own history for their own people.[102]

★

Any objective and carefully prepared account of the history
of Vietnam must conclude with the fact that the United States
must bear the responsibility for the torture of an entire nation
since the end of the Second World War. The return of France
to Vietnam, and its ability to fight for the restoration of a
colony, was due to critical political decisions made in Washington in 1945, and the later repression depended on financial
and military aid given to France by the United States. First as
a passive senior partner, and then as the primary party, the
United States made Vietnam an international arena for the
Cold War, and it is a serious error to regard the war in Vietnam as a civil conflict, or even secondarily as a by-product of

132 The ROOTS OF AMERICAN FOREIGN POLICY

one—for in that form it would hardly have lasted very long against a national and radical movement that the vast majority of the Vietnamese people always have sustained.

The United States Government responded to its chronic inability to find a viable internal alternative to the Vietminh and the N.L.F. by escalating the war against virtually the entire nation. To escape certain defeat time and time again, it violated formal and customary international law by increasing the scale of military activity. The United States met each overture to negotiate, whether it came from the Vietnamese, the French, or the Russians, by accelerated warfare in the hope of attaining its unique ends through military means rather than diplomacy.

Ultimately, the United States has fought in Vietnam with increasing intensity to extend its hegemony over the world community and to stop every form of revolutionary movement which refuses to accept the predominant role of the United States in the direction of the affairs of its nation or region. Repeatedly defeated in Vietnam in the attainment of its impossible objective, the United States Government, having alienated most of its European allies and a growing sector of its own nation, is attempting to prove to itself and the world that it remains indeed strong enough to define the course of global politics despite the opposition of a small, poor nation of peasants. On the outcome of this epic contest rests the future of peace and social progress in the world for the remainder of the twentieth century, not just for those who struggle to overcome the legacy of colonialism and oppression to build new lives, but for the people of the United States themselves.

EPILOGUE: ON REASON AND RADICALISM

ANY SERIOUS ANALYSIS of the United States role in the world today will inevitably reveal much more of the permanent interests, profitability, and coherence underlying contemporary American foreign policy. And not only will it show the rationality of Washington's actions in perpetuating American power, even against the wishes of large and growing numbers of Americans, but also the relative durability of a policy increasingly difficult to apply successfully as it taxes the nation along with the world. For if consensus is ultimately based on the possibility of enforced conformity, as expressed often in this century in the history of the suppression of civil liberties, then the magnitude of the tasks facing Americans seeking a fundamental change in this society's global role is proportionately greater.

It is in fact the lack of a serious diagnosis and analysis of the American social order, either from the Left—new or old —or from the scholarly community, that makes possible the illusion that what opponents of the *status quo* confront is an ephemeral miscarriage of a sense of justice inherent in the larger, historic direction of American society at home and abroad. Yet what I have attempted to document and argue in this volume is that both the practical and intellectual tasks challenging advocates of profound change in American policy —of which I am one—are far more complex. It is this illusion of the "accidental" quality of the role of the United States in Vietnam and elsewhere that has led over the past years to a kind of specious liberalism which believes one simply replaces individuals in office with other men, such as a Kennedy or McCarthy, rather than solving problems with an altogether new system based on a radically different distribution of power and assumptions as to its application. And this capricious view has also resulted in an only slightly more sophisticated form of "radicalism" or New Leftism based on confrontation tactics, often including civil disobedience, which vaguely assumes that a form of rational discourse is possible by emphatic protest and reason speaking to, and somehow transforming, power.

Yet the assumption of marching in front of the Pentagon or the Democratic convention implies that the existing system can be something other than what it is short of actually depriving it of access to power and levers for controlling society, and that the beneficiaries of power will not ruthlessly apply their resources should, for example, the protesters lock arms and sweep through the White House. In brief, such a strategy not only avoids the central question of the logic and imperatives of Washington's course at home and abroad, but it is also poor social analysis both for descriptive and prescriptive purposes. For one cannot build a description of American society today merely by acting without first also considering the premises and relevance of one's conduct, save if there is limitless time for interminable failures on the part of the opponents to the dominant course of history—a luxury that has never existed in this century.

To some critical extent, and as difficult as that task may be, sustained structural analysis and theory must precede commitment in depth to one or another mode of tactics and action. This is especially true, as in the case of most recent liberal and radical protest, when the opposition base their actions on the illusions of the existence of "freedom" in this form of consensual society, thereby also unthinkingly strengthening elite-encouraged mythologies concerning the nature of the political process or the efficacy of moral pleas.

Social protest is most preferably useful *and* truthful, but if we must temporarily sacrifice action to principle we will in the long run be far better off thereby. For no one has ever shown, either in this country or in Western Europe, how the politics of "responsibility" and the insistence on activity for its own sake have transformed a useful myth that men can alter power with petitions or reason to end profitable if profoundly dangerous and destructive policies on the part of their rulers. And if the opportunistic cultivation of functional illusions has led only to the abdication of identity and integrity on the part of nominal opponents of the *status quo,* and scarcely the slightest alteration of existing society, then even the pragmatic criterion for sacrificing truth, however temporarily, fails.

One need not so much deplore liberal opportunism or mindless radical heroism as to find them lacking by their own measures, for they end nowhere, and in the case of some of the aesthetic modes of recent New Left protest they irresistibly lead to an increasingly intense personalism and cult of escapism as more and more suffer the shock of recognizing that existing power and rulers are quite as firmly entrenched despite their exposure to personally "liberated" individuals or their dialogues with moralists. Yet without some coherent analysis and a theory based upon it there are no clearly defined limits to action, no restraints to capitulations or moral failures, and no definite assumptions upon which one bases one's response to an evil society and its conduct. This lack of directing standards opens the door both to opportunism and to romanticism. Yet, on the other hand, analysis and theory divorced from possible modes of active human responses to social conditions can, in the long run, lead to the reduction of these most vital human problems to a sterile academic level whose ultimate posterity will be in footnotes rather than in the transformation of the social structure—it can duplicate the fate of contemporary sociology.

Yet it is that delicate willingness alone to pass over to a stage of critical thoughtfulness and temporary isolation from the existing conservative political process, and to act decisively when the never-predictable moment comes, that holds out any hope for radicals having an impact in the industrialized world. For however frustrating tactical withdrawal from illusory and fruitless action may be, especially for an opposition that feels it must act for its own sake even if the assumptions of that action generate new myths or legitimize old ones, the fact remains that true and durable political commitment can come only from a much greater degree of clarity than presently exists among those who reject the leadership and goals of America's men of power. In a minimal way, this means defining necessary if not sufficient conditions and assumptions for the transformation of the direction of American society, to discover its limits, possibilities, and dynamics, and to subject the necessarily unknown more to reason than to a faith in the possibility of sudden utopian salvation.

Such a course foregoes optimism or pessimism, but rather requires realism concerning the weaknesses and potential of existing American power at home and abroad, and its capacity for transformation. America, in this view, is both dreams and traps, and all that is certain is that the structure of the world makes it only inevitable that America will change. What is cause for pessimism is the fact that the main beneficiaries of American power show not the slightest hesitancy in acting decisively to retain or magnify their power at home and abroad—they have, in brief, both a will and a still substantial capacity to survive. For this reason one must regard their inability to succeed in their Vietnamese undertaking as not necessarily decisive to internal change but merely as a critical factor that sharpens and reveals the integrative limits of the existing order of power. It might lead, at least for a time, to successful repression at home even as it becomes less and less possible abroad.

In its own perverse manner, the need of men of power to restrain internal dissent and opposition would reveal elements warranting long-term optimism, for it would also necessarily reflect a deepening and growing rupture between leaders and the led, and expose more fully the realities upon which power is based. And since this existing consensus-from-above is tenuous during every crisis period, it would expose the unwillingness of more and more Americans to tolerate their political impotence, ever higher taxes, and the sustained draft and death of their sons. For even, as seems likely, if Vietnam is joined or followed by more interventions elsewhere, the capacity and willingness of the American people to cooperate with, much less endorse, such a course is now seriously in doubt. It is at that point of refusal only that American political dynamics will result in a condition of both great dangers and possibilities.

In this context, while the Vietnam war continues, or while men everywhere in the Third World resist American efforts at domination, the United States internal dynamics are profoundly affected, and the rest of the world is forced to do for the American people what they are only tangentially presently able and willing to do for themselves. The victims of American executioners, ironically, thereby work not only for their own integrity and freedom but indirectly for that of the American people themselves. In return, this dialectic requires Americans with a better vision of their own future to understand their profound debts to liberation movements everywhere, and in Vietnam most of all, and while refusing personal complicity with the war in every possible manner they must also recognize that so long as American power responds only to power, and is contained only by its own limitations and inability to succeed, the fate of the Vietnamese resistance will fundamentally affect the possibilities of the American people ultimately to escape the deadly trap of the Cold War. And its failure will be far more significant than all the liberal pleas or radical "moral" confrontations with immoral men in defining the thrust of American life and energies in the coming decades.

Once the conditioning and limitation of American power have occurred in the foreign sphere, creating new options in the economy and society at home, the role of the domestic opponents of irrationality and the system that creates it will depend on their own wisdom and resources, wisdom that is hopefully already colored by a thoroughgoing honesty even if it appears at times to be composed of irrelevance, negativism, and destructive criticism. To prepare with clarity today for that future is a long overdue and imperative function of American intellectuals committed to radical humanist change. To transform society they must first understand it, its structure and purposes, its toughness and weakness, and define appropriate means and tactics of change which seriously take these durable realities into account. And even if such an articulation of tactics, principles, and goals is hardly an exclusive or sufficient activity in the total process of future history, action today based on convenient and comforting myths and assumptions beclouds the clear vision that will be required when profound social change is again possible in the United States.

NOTES

Chapter 1. Men of Power

1. I have attempted to trace the origins of modern federal bureaucracy and power in my book, *The Triumph of Conservatism* (Chicago, 1967 [paperback ed.]); I have outlined the economic context of power in my *Wealth and Power in America* (New York, 1962).

2. Paul A. Smith, "Opinions, Publics, and World Affairs in the United States," *Western Political Quarterly,* XIV (September 1961), 698–714; Martin Kriesberg, "Dark Areas of Ignorance," in *Public Opinion and Foreign Relations,* Lester Markel, ed. (New York, 1949), 49–64; Gabriel A. Almond, *The American People and Foreign Policy* (New York, 1950), 85 ff.

3. Martin B. Hickman and Neil Hollander, "Undergraduate Origin as a Factor in Elite Recruitment and Mobility: The Foreign Service—A Case Study," *Western Political Quarterly,* XIX (June 1966), 337–42; W. Lloyd Warner *et al., The American Federal Executive* (New Haven, 1963), 14–129, 163; David T. Stanley, Dean E. Mann, and Jameson W. Doig, *Men Who Govern: A Biographical Profile of Federal Political Executives* (Washington, 1967), 126.

4. C. Wright Mills, *The Power Elite* (New York, 1956), 28–29,

288–96, and *passim; United States News,* May 23, 1947, 20–21; "Who Really Runs the State Department . . . ," *U.S. News and World Report,* May 5, 1950, 32–33; Warner, *et al., American Federal Executive,* 163; G. William Domhoff, *Who Rules America?* (Englewood Cliffs, N.J., 1967); Paul M. Sweezy, "Power Elite or Ruling Class?" in *C. Wright Mills and the Power Elite,* G. William Domhoff and Hoyt B. Ballard, eds. (Boston, 1968), 115–32, for the best critique of Mills.

5. Note on Methods. We examined four Cabinet-level Departments for the period 1944–60: the State, War and Defense, Treasury, and Commerce Departments, their Secretaries, Under and Assistant Secretaries, and Special Assistants to the Secretaries. We included this last-named post because these officials are traditionally the links between the Cabinet members and major problems. In addition, we examined positions designated "Deputy" or "Special" Secretary, Under or Assistant Secretary.

Also surveyed were the Army, Air Force, and Navy Departments, which have similar organizational structures. The other agencies, however, are organized along different lines, and it was possible only to estimate the equivalents of Cabinet posts. Only a random selection of the highest officers is included in the case of the White House staff, the military governments of Germany and Japan, and the E.C.A.-M.S.A.-I.C.A. foreign aid organizations, while the aid organizations incorporate a number of lower level officials. Moreover, the category of "Miscellaneous Government Departments" includes *all* the key individuals' Government posts—in the agencies indicated or others—that do not otherwise qualify for study. The net effect of this technique is to minimize slightly the percentage of posts individuals with law or business backgrounds held. In brief, these data are conservative estimates of the extent of private control of public office.

The data on career backgrounds and history may be found in various issues of *Moody's Industrials, Moody's Manual of Investments, Poor's Register of Directors and Executives, Who's Who, Who Was Who, Martindale-Hubble Legal Directory, Congressional Directory,* and the *New York Times.*

6. My preceding data were collected in 1966, and in September 1967 the Brookings Institution published *Men Who Govern,* by David T. Stanley, Dean E. Mann, and Jameson W. Doig. The Brookings volume is far superior to any hitherto published study and is unmarred by debilitating ideological biases masked as methodology. It covers 1,041 individuals who held 1,567 key executive appointments from March 1933 to April 1965. These included persons who attained posts—nearly one-third the total—too low to be included in my sample, another one-quarter were Kennedy-Johnson appointees, and somewhat less than this figure served prior to 1944. The authors included all Cabinet-level positions, while I included only four Cabinet agencies. My sample, therefore, covers a more select group of leaders over a shorter time span.

The authors of the Brookings study show that 39 percent of their 1,041 leaders received a private preparatory education, with 60 percent, 46 percent, and 44 percent for the State, Treasury, and Defense Departments, respectively. Nineteen percent attended Yale, Harvard, or Princeton. Twenty-four percent of *all* appointees were principally businessmen before appointment, this figure reaching 40 percent for the Cabinet Secretaries, 56 percent for Military Secretaries, and 42 percent for Under Secretaries. Twenty-six percent of all appointees were lawyers, though the Brookings study does not explore the size or nature of their firms. Sixty-three percent of all Cabinet Secretaries, 86 percent of the Military Secretaries, 66 percent of all Under Secretaries, and 50 percent of all Assistant Secretaries were either businessmen or lawyers prior to political appointment, generally corroborating my findings for a more selective sample.

Including ranks lower than those I considered, the Brookings study revealed that 16 percent of their State Department sample, 1933–65, were principally businessmen before their appointments, and this figure grew to 39 percent in Defense, 57 percent in Commerce, and 60 percent in the Navy Department. While businessmen and lawyers accounted for 60 percent of the Eisenhower appointees, the Johnson Administration had the lowest, at 40 percent. President Johnson also appointed more men with master's and doctoral degrees than any of his predecessors, which only tends to prove my contention that the origins of individuals are less responsible for the continuity of the policies of the nation than most critics have cared to admit.

Manufacturing provided 44 percent of the persons designated as businessmen, finance 23 percent, and other forms of capital the remainder. Defense contractors provided 12 percent of the executives considered in the defense-related agencies, reaching a peak of one-fifth under Kennedy. If one removes retirements, deaths, and other statistical imbalances, nearly half the State Department executives had subsequent business and private professional careers, mainly in law, this percentage reaching over three-quarters for most of the other agencies included in my sample.

7. Telephone conversation between James F. Forrestal and Reese H. Taylor, March 25, 1947, in James F. Forrestal Papers, Princeton University Library, box 73. See also Forrestal memo to Dean Acheson, May 17, 1947, Forrestal Papers, box 70, for an example of how this was done.

8. *New York Times,* June 26, 1966.

9. *Business Week,* April 14, 1945, 18–19.

10. U.S. House, Committee on the Judiciary, *Hearings, WOC's and Government Advisory Groups.* 84:1–2 (Washington, 1955–56), 1570 ff., 2267–2580. See Paul W. Cherington and Ralph L. Gillen, *The Business Representative in Washington* (Washington, 1962), *passim;* Robert Engler, *The Politics of Oil* (New York, 1961), 310–17.

11. U.S. House, Committee on the Judiciary, *Interim Report of the Anti-trust Subcommittee . . . on WOC's and Government Advisory Groups.* 84:2. April 24, 1956. (Washington, 1956), 8–16, 29, 56–62, 90, 143, 150, 161–62; Committee on the Judiciary, *WOC's and Government Advisory Groups,* 282–83, 521 ff., 1878–2146; for an excellent summary, see Michael D. Reagan, "The Business and Defense Services Administration, 1953–57," *Western Political Quarterly,* XIV (June 1961), 569–86.

Chapter 2. The American Military and Civil Authority

1. Harold D. Lasswell, *National Security and Individual Freedom* (New York, 1950), chap. II. See also Harold D. Lasswell, "The Garrison-State Hypothesis Today," in *Changing Patterns of Military Politics,* Samuel P. Huntington, ed. (New York, 1962), 51–70.

2. C. Wright Mills, *The Power Elite* (New York, 1956), 28, 198–201, 214–15, 274–78, 292–96.

3. Paul A. C. Koistinen, "The 'Industrial-Military' Complex in Historical Perspective: World War I," *Business History Review,* XLI (Winter 1967), 378–403; Albert A. Blum, "Birth and Death of the M-Day Plan," in *American Civil-Military Decisions,* Harold Stein, ed. (Montgomery, Ala., 1963), 63 ff.; Samuel P. Huntington, *The Soldier and the State: The Theory and Politics of Civil-Military Relations* (Cambridge, 1957), 315–16; Eliot Janeway, *The Struggle for Survival: A Chronicle of Economic Mobilization in World War II* (New Haven, 1951), 59–70.

4. Quoted in Samuel P. Huntington, "Interservice Competition and the Political Roles of the Armed Services," *American Political Science Review,* LV (March 1961), 47.

5. Merton J. Peck and Frederic M. Scherer, *The Weapons Acquisition Process: An Economic Analysis* (Boston, 1962), 237 n, 342, 366, 535–36; Charles N. Bernstein, "How to Propose a Research Program," *Missiles and Rockets,* VI (April 18, 1960), 32; Samuel P. Huntington, *The Common Defense: Strategic Programs in National Politics* (New York, 1961), 397–402; U.S. House, Committee on Armed Services, *Report . . . on Employment of Retired Commissioned Officers by Defense Department Contractors.* 86:1 (Washington, 1960), 16.

6. *Army-Navy-Air Force Journal,* April 16, 1960, 921. See also U.S. House, *Report . . . on Employment of Retired Commissioned Officers,* 9–13; U.S. House, Committee on Armed Services, *Supplemental Hearings Released from Executive Session Relating to Entertainment Furnished by the Martin Company of Baltimore,*

Md., of U.S. Government Officers. 86:1. September 10, 1959 (Washington, 1959), 29, 42 ff.

7. *Army-Navy-Air Force Journal,* September 24, 1955, 91. See also Mills, *The Power Elite,* 174, 196, 222; Huntington, *Soldier and the State, passim;* Morris Janowitz, *Sociology and the Military Establishment* (New York, 1959), *passim; New York Times,* January 18, 1961, 22; Gen. Omar N. Bradley to Gen. Douglas MacArthur, May 20, 1948, and Memo on "Army Policy on Discussion of Russia," November 19, 1947, in Douglas MacArthur Papers, MacArthur Memorial Library, Norfolk, Va., Record Group 5; Gen. Omar N. Bradley, in *Department of State Bulletin,* XXVIII (March 16, 1953), 414–15; Huntington, *The Common Defense,* 47–53.

8. Gen. Matthew B. Ridgway, *Soldier: Memoirs of Matthew B. Ridgway* (New York, 1956), 270.

9. *New York Times,* October 29, 1961.

10. *Time,* September 4, 1950, 12; Harry S Truman, *Memoirs* (Garden City, N.Y., 1956), II, 383. See also U.S. Senate, Committee on Government Operations, *Hearings, Organizing for National Security.* 87:1. January 1960 (Washington, 1961), 1206–09; U.S. Senate, Committee on Armed Services, *Hearings, Military Cold War Education and Speech Review Policies.* 87:2. January 1962 (Washington, 1962), *passim; New York Times,* January 28, June 18, November 1, 1961; U.S. Senate, *Congressional Record,* August 2, 1961, 13436–42.

11. *New York Times,* September 1, 1950, 3; *Time,* September 11, 1950, 22.

12. Peck and Scherer, *Weapons Acquisition Process,* 100; Paul Y. Hammond, "Supercarriers and B-36 Bombers: Appropriations Strategy and Politics," in *American Civil-Military Decisions,* 481–91; Huntington, "Interservice Competition and the Political Roles of the Armed Services," 41; Truman, *Memoirs,* 53.

13. U.S. House, Committee on Armed Services, *Hearings, Investigation of the B-36 Bomber Program.* 81:1. August–October 1949 (Washington, 1949), 13–20, 51–84, 477–92, 626–33.

14. U.S. House, Committee on Armed Services, *Hearings, The*

National Defense Program—Unification and Strategy. 81:1. October 1949 (Washington, 1949), 51, 56, 403, 436. See also *ibid.,* 45, 104, 185–89, 207–12, 238–41.

15. *Ibid.,* 518. See also Truman, *Memoirs,* 53; Hammond, "Supercarriers and B-36 Bombers," 547.

16. U.S. House, *The National Defense Program,* 516–21, 545, 565, 638; Werner R. Schilling, Paul Y. Hammond, and Glenn H. Snyder, *Strategy, Politics, and Defense Budgets* (New York, 1962), 7–263; Elias Huzar, *The Purse and the Sword: Control of the Army by Congress Through Military Appropriations, 1933–1950* (Ithaca, 1950), *passim;* Huntington, *Soldier and the State,* 420–21; Huntington, *The Common Defense,* 387–91.

17. David E. Lilienthal, *The Journals of David E. Lilienthal: The Atomic Energy Years, 1945–1950* (New York, 1964), 351; Truman, *Memoirs,* 59; U.S. Senate, *Organizing for National Security,* I, 154, 161–62, 563, 573, 673–74, 685, II, 431–33.

18. Truman, *Memoirs,* 309; Huntington, *The Common Defense,* 47–53, 64–98; Schilling *et al., Strategy, Politics, and Defense Budgets,* 275–362, 400–76; Ridgway, *Soldier,* 272–77; U.S. Senate, *Organizing for National Security,* I, 797–98.

19. Mills, *The Power Elite,* 199.

20. Peck and Scherer, *Weapons Acquisition Process,* 72–73; Gene N. Lyons, "The New Civil-Military Relations," *American Political Science Review,* LV (March 1961), 54–55; Burton M. Sapin and Richard C. Snyder, *The Role of the Military in American Foreign Policy* (Garden City, N.Y., 1954), 26–30; Huntington, *The Common Defense,* 115, 155–57.

21. General Dwight D. Eisenhower, Memo, "Scientific and Technological Resources as Military Assets," April 27, 1946, Henry L. Stimson Papers, Yale University Library.

22. U.S. House, Committee on Government Operations, *Hearings, Organization and Management of Missile Programs.* 86:1. February–March 1959 (Washington, 1959), 504, 671–74, 689–96, 716, 731–33, 742, 753, 758, 767–69, 775–77; U.S. House, Committee on Government Operations, *Report on Organization and Management of Missile Programs.* 86:1. September 2, 1959

(Washington, 1959), 69–141; U.S. House, Committee on Armed Services, *Hearings, Weapons System Management and Team System Concept in Government Contracting.* 86:1. April–August 1959 (Washington, 1959), 27–29, 563–67.

23. U.S. Senate, *Organizing for National Security,* I, 1190.

24. U.S. Senate, Committee on Armed Services, *Hearings, Military Cold War Education and Speech Review Policies.* 87:2. January 1962 (Washington, 1962), 9–12; *Business Week,* July 13, 1963, 56–90; *Wall Street Journal,* March 20, 1961, February 19, 1962; *New York Times,* March 2, 1962, September 5, October 8, 1963, February 2, 1965.

Chapter 3. The United States and World Economic Power

1. Forrestal statement, December 3, 1947, in President's Air Policy Commission Papers, Harry S Truman Library, Independence, Mo., box 17.

2. U.S. Senate, Committee on Banking and Currency, *Hearings, International Development Association.* 85:2. March 1958 (Washington, 1958), 69.

3. U.S. Senate, Committee on Interior and Insular Affairs, *Report, Accessibility of Strategic and Critical Materials to the United States in Time of War and for Our Expanding Economy.* 83:2. July 9, 1954 (Washington, 1954), 1. See also statements of Paul H. Nitze in *Department of State Bulletin,* February 26, 1947, 300, and November 21, 1948, 626–27; Department of State, *The United States and Africa* (Washington, 1964), *passim; New York Times,* August 18, 1963; Percy W. Bidwell, *Raw Materials: A Study of American Policy* (New York, 1958), 2, 6; Hans H. Landsberg, Leonard L. Fischman, and Joseph L. Fisher, *Resources in America's Future: Patterns of Requirements and Availabilities, 1960– 2000* (Baltimore, 1963), 427. Certain of these themes for the period 1943–45 are explored in detail in my *The Politics of War* (New York, 1968), and for 1946–55 in a forthcoming history of the period my wife and I are presently writing.

4. Landsberg *et al., Resources in America's Future,* 45. See also *ibid.,* 15.

5. *Ibid.,* 428; *New York Times,* April 17, 1966; *The Economist,* June 5, 1965, 1155; General Agreement on Tariffs and Trade [GATT], *Trends in International Trade: A Report by a Panel of Experts* (Geneva, 1958), 43; Paul Bairoch, *Diagnostic de l'Évolution Économique du Tiers-Monde, 1900–1966* (Paris, 1967), 76; U.S. President's Materials Policy Commission, *Resources for Freedom,* June 1952 (Washington, 1952), I, 9. Bairoch's book is the best available study on the relationship of the Third World to the world economy.

6. Landsberg *et al., Resources in America's Future,* 430, 437, 440, 443, 448, 456, 459, 464, 466, 468.

7. *Survey of Current Business,* September 1967, 36; U.S. Bureau of Census, *1963 Census of Manufacturers* (Washington, 1966), I, II, Part II, *passim;* Landsberg *et al., Resources in America's Future,* 474–76, 882, 901, 904, 906, 912.

8. United Nations Conference on Trade and Development [UNCTAD], "Review of International Trade and Development, 1967: Part 1 . . ." November 15, 1967 (mimeo, 1967), 19. Bairoch gives the figures as 31.8 percent in 1948 and 22.1 percent in 1966. Bairoch, *Diagnostic,* 123. 1966 was therefore the lowest share since 1913. See also Inter-American Development Bank, Social Progress Trust Fund, *Seventh Annual Report, 1967* (Washington, 1968), 6.

9. Bairoch, *Diagnostic,* 123, 132; UNCTAD, "Review of International Trade and Development," 20; *Board of Trade Journal,* 193 (October 27, 1967), vii; U.S. Department of Commerce, *U.S. Share of World Markets for Manufactured Products, Analysis of Changes from 1954 Through 1961* (Washington, 1964), 8; U.S. Department of Commerce, *International Commerce,* 73 (June 5, 1967), 24; Anne Romanis, "Relative Growth of Exports of Manufacturers of the United States and Other Industrial Countries," *International Monetary Fund Staff Papers,* May 1961, 241–73; Research and Statistics Department, International Monetary Fund, "Changes in the Trade Balances of Industrial Countries," March 10, 1967; *International Commerce,* 73 (December 11, 1967), 6–7.

10. U.S. Department of Agriculture, *Handbook of Agricultural*

Charts, 1967 (Washington, 1967), 40–41, 48; Department of State, *The United States Economy and the Mutual Security Program* (Washington, 1959), 21; Department of Commerce, National Export Expansion Council, "Report of Task Force 1 . . . ," [ms] (1967?), 10–11.

11. Bairoch, *Diagnostic,* 160–65; United Nations, Department of Economic and Social Affairs, *Yearbook of International Trade Statistics, 1965* (New York, 1967), 33–34; UNCTAD, "Commodity Problems and Policies," November 10, 1967 (mimeo, 1967), 4, 9; GATT, *International Trade, 1966: GATT-Report 1967* (Geneva, 1967), 2–3, 9, 43, 47, 50; UNCTAD, "Review of International Trade and Development," 35–36.

12. Percy W. Bidwell, "Raw Materials and National Policy," *Foreign Affairs,* XXXVII (October 1958), 152–53; *Le Monde,* October 19, 1966, 20; H. W. Singer, "The Distribution of Gains Between Investing and Borrowing Countries," *American Economic Review,* XL (May 1950), 473–85; Bairoch, *Diagnostic,* 28, 79–83, 88–95, 104, 203; United Nations, Department of Economic and Social Affairs, *The Growth of World Industry, 1938–1961: International Analyses and Tables* (New York, 1965), 234; GATT, *International Trade, 1966,* 56, 58; Inter-American Development Bank, Social Progress Trust Fund, *Fourth Annual Report, 1964* (Washington, 1965), 108.

13. Lamar Fleming to Dwight D. Eisenhower, November 19, 1958, Dwight D. Eisenhower Papers, OF116-J, Eisenhower Library, Abilene, Kansas. See also U.S. Senate, Committee on Foreign Relations, *United States-Latin American Relations* ["Compilation of Studies"], 86:2. August 31, 1960 (Washington, 1960), 438–44; UNCTAD, "Commodity Problems and Policies," 19; International Economic Consultants, *Commodity Problems in Latin America,* prepared for U.S. Senate, Committee on Foreign Relations, 86:1. December 12, 1959 (Washington, 1959), 58.

14. M. S. Venkataramani, "Manganese as a Factor in Indo-American Relations," *India Quarterly,* XIV (April–June 1958), 140. See also UNCTAD, "Commodity Problems and Policies," 19–20; *Wall Street Journal,* January 30, 1958, October 24, 1967;

New York Times, April 14, July 5, August 24, September 24, December 7, 9, 1964, March 31, 1966; National Planning Association, *The Foreign Aid Programs and the United States Economy,* prepared for U.S. Senate, Special Committee to Study Foreign Aid Program, 85:1 (Washington, 1957), 812–13; President's Materials Policy Commission, *Resources for Freedom,* V, 120; *Business Week,* September 18, 1948, 25–26, December 16, 1950, 26.

15. Quoted in Charles Wolf, Jr., *Foreign Aid: Theory and Practice in Southern Asia* (Princeton, 1960), 265. See also Venkataramani, "Manganese as a Factor in Indo-American Relations," 150; Bidwell, *Raw Materials,* 352.

16. U.S. Senate, Committee on Armed Services, *Report, Inquiry into the Strategic and Critical Material Stockpiles of the United States.* 88:1. October 24, 1963 (Washington, 1963), 1–14; *New York Times,* October 12, 1963.

17. Committee on Foreign Relations, *United States-Latin American Relations,* 472. See also *ibid.,* 127–30, 176–81, 471, 531–32; U.S. Congress, Joint Economic Committee, *Hearings, Latin American Development and Western Hemisphere Trade.* 89:1. September 1965 (Washington, 1965), 134; Henry Brodie, *Commodity Agreements: A Partial Answer to the Trade Problems of Developing Countries* [Department of State Publication 7935] (Washington, 1965), 4, 10.

18. Quoted in Simon G. Hanson, "The International Coffee Agreement," *Inter-American Economic Affairs,* XVII (Autumn 1963), 91.

19. For coffee, see *ibid.,* 75–94; *New York Times,* December 22, 1963, February 26, March 6, 1964, February 20, 1968; for sugar, see U.S. Senate, Committee on Foreign Relations, *Hearings, International Sugar Agreement.* 83:2. March 18, 1954 (Washington, 1954), *passim.*

20. Department of Agriculture, *Handbook of Agricultural Charts,* 42, 48; U.S. Congress, Joint Economic Committee, *Hearings, Outlook for United States Balance of Payments.* 87:2. December 1962 (Washington, 1963), 63; Department of State, *United States Economy and the Mutual Security Program,* 66, 80; Com-

mittee on Foreign Relations, *United States-Latin American Relations,* 445, 455; National Export Expansion Council, "Report of Task Force 1 . . . ," 10; National Export Expansion Council, *Trade and Investment in Developing Countries* (Washington, April 3, 1967), 11.

21. R. R. Adams, Task Group 4, "Encouragement of U.S. Industrial Activity in Underdeveloped Countries," April 27, 1959, in James E. Webb Papers, Truman Library, box 29. See also George Humphrey to Dwight D. Eisenhower, May 7, 1956, Eisenhower Papers, OF116-B; U.S. Congress, Joint Economic Committee, *Hearings, Employment, Growth, and Price Levels.* 86:1. June–July 1959 (Washington, 1959), 906; *New York Times,* December 22, 1963; U.S. President's Committee to Study the United States Military Assistance Program, *Third Interim Report, Economic Assistance Programs and Administration* (Washington, 1959), 27–28; U.S. House, Committee on Foreign Affairs, *Hearings, Foreign Assistance Act of 1966.* 89:2. March 1966 (Washington, 1966), 85.

22. Speech of John F. Kennedy, September 17, 1963, White House Press Release, 4. See also National Planning Association, *Foreign Aid Programs,* 813; *New York Times,* April 12, 1964.

23. *New York Times,* March 30, 1966. See also Joint Economic Committee, *Outlook for United States Balance of Payments,* 62–69; U.S. President's Citizen Advisors on the Mutual Security Program, *Report to the President,* March 1, 1957 (Washington, 1957), 7–19.

24. U.S. Agency for International Development, *Loan Terms, Debt Burden and Development* (Washington, April 1965), 40; "Total Debt-Service Payments During 1967," March 20, 1968 [unpublished data kindly given to me by the Department of State]; Inter-American Development Bank, *Seventh Annual Report, 1967,* 25. See also A.I.D., *Loan Terms, Debt Burden, passim,* for data cited above, and Joint Economic Committee, *Latin American Development,* 142–43.

25. U.S. Department of Commerce, *U.S. Business Investments in Foreign Countries* (Washington, 1960), 60–64, 90, 92, 139; Emilio G. Collado and Jack F. Bennett, "Private Investment and

Economic Development," *Foreign Affairs,* XXXV (July 1957), 633–34; *Survey of Current Business,* September 1967, 40, 45, 49; Committee on Foreign Relations, *United States-Latin American Relations,* 511; *New York Times,* November 17, 1963.

26. Department of Commerce, *U.S. Business Investments,* 43, 65–66; *The Economist,* July 10, 1965, 167; Allan W. Johnstone, *United States Direct Investment in France* (Cambridge, 1965), 48–49; *Le Monde,* January 14–15, July 23, 1968; *Wall Street Journal,* December 12, 1967; Committee on Foreign Relations, *United States–Latin American Relations,* 338; *New York Times,* April 16, 1968.

27. *Survey of Current Business,* September 1967, 45, 48; Committee on Foreign Relations, *United States–Latin America Relations,* 306; *The Exchange,* January 1963, 7–14; National Export Expansion Council, *Trade and Investment,* 11; *The Economist,* February 13, 1965, 669; Department of Commerce, *Balance of Payments: Statistical Supplement, Revised Edition* (Washington, 1963), 183–84.

28. Department of Commerce, *Balance of Payments,* 120, 150–51.

29. U.S. International Cooperation Administration, Press Release Number 338, September 12, 1957.

30. Douglas Dillon to Joseph M. Dodge, September 16, 1958, Joseph M. Dodge Papers, Detroit Public Library, Misc. Files, box 1. See also George Humphrey to Dwight D. Eisenhower, May 7, 1956, Eisenhower Papers, OF116-B; George M. Humphrey to Joseph M. Dodge, September 17, 1958, Dodge Papers, Misc. Files, box 1.

31. George M. Humphrey to Paul G. Hoffman, March 26, 1957, Eisenhower Papers, OF116-B.

32. Bidwell, "Raw Materials and National Policy," 153.

33. Eugene R. Black, *The Diplomacy of Economic Development* (Cambridge, 1960), 53.

34. U.S. Congress, Joint Economic Committee, *Economic Policies and Programs in South America.* 87:2 (Washington, 1962), 25; Joint Economic Committee, *Latin American Development,*

10–11, 25–26, 30, 81, 179, 194; statements of Lucius Clay and George Moore in *General Electric Forum,* VI (October–December 1963), 32–33; VII (January–March 1964), 6–8; U.S. Congress, Joint Economic Committee, *Report, Economic Developments in South America.* 87:2 (Washington, 1962), 6; H. G. Grubel and A. D. Scott, "The Immigration of Scientists and Engineers to the United States," *Journal of Political Economy,* LXXIV (August 1966), 368–78; *New York Times,* March 18, 22, 26, 1964, April 10, 1966, March 7, May 2, 1967, March 9, 1968; Department of State, Office of External Research, *Foreign Student Exchange in Perspective* (Washington, 1968), 14–20; Committee on Foreign Relations, *United States–Latin American Relations,* 467–68; Thomas Balogh, *Unequal Partners: The Theoretical Framework* (Oxford, 1963), 32.

35. *New York Times,* April 3, 1964. See also *New York Times,* May 29, 30, June 3, October 30, November 11, 12, 14, 16, 1963; April 7, December 24, 1964.

36. A. C. Ingraham memo of August 13, 1956, in *Congressional Record,* 85:1. February 22, 1957, 2181–82.

37. U.S. House, Committee on Foreign Affairs, *Staff Memorandum on International Lending and Guarantee Programs.* 88:2. December 21, 1964 (Washington, 1964), 63–65; U.S. Congress, Joint Economic Committee, *Report, Private Investment in Latin America.* 88:2. May 25, 1964 (Washington, 1964), 3, 6, 18; *New York Times,* July 31, 1964.

38. John Gallagher and Ronald Robinson, "The Imperialism of Free Trade," *Economic History Review,* Second Series, VI (August 1953), 5–6.

Chapter 4. The United States in Vietnam, 1944–66:
Origins and Objectives

1. U.S. Department of State, *Foreign Relations of the United States: 1943* (Washington, 1963), III, 37; Department of State, *Foreign Relations of the United States: The Conferences at Cairo and Tehran* (Washington, 1961), 485.

2. Department of State, *Foreign Relations of the United States: 1945* (Washington, 1967), I, 124; Department of State, *Foreign Relations of the United States: The Conference of Berlin* (Washington, 1960), I, 920.

3. Charles De Gaulle, *Memoires de Guerre: Le Salut, 1944–1946.* Livres de Poche ed. (Paris, 1964), 467–68; Department of State, *Foreign Relations of the United States: 1945* (Washington, 1968), IV, 704.

4. General G. Sabattier, *Le Destin de l'Indochine* (Paris, 1952), 336–38.

5. Gen. Philip Gallagher to Gen. R. B. McClure, Sept. 20, 1945, Gallagher Papers, Office of the Chief of Military History, U.S. Army, Washington, D.C.

6. Department of State, Research and Intelligence Service, "Biographical Information on Prominent Nationalist Leaders in French Indochina." R. & A. 3336. Oct. 25, 1945 (no place); State Department Report, October 15–28, 1945, in Gallagher Papers.

7. United Kingdom, Secretary of State for Foreign Affairs, *Documents Relating to British Involvement in the Indo-China Conflict, 1945–1965.* Cmnd. 2834 (London, 1965), 50; see also F. S. V. Donnison, *British Military Administration in the Far East, 1943–46* (London, 1957), 404–08.

8. State Department Report in Gallagher Papers, 10.

9. *New York Times* (hereafter *NYT*), Feb. 8, 1947. See also Bernard B. Fall, *The Two Viet-Nams* (New York, 1963), 75–76.

10. Marvin E. Gettleman, ed., *Vietnam: History, Documents, and Opinions on a Major World Crisis* (New York, 1965), 79.

11. U.S. Senate, Committee on Foreign Relations, *Hearings: Nomination of Philip C. Jessup.* 82:1 (Washington, 1951), 603.

12. Department of State, "Conference on Problems of United States Policy in China. Oct. 6–8, 1949." [Transcript of Proceedings] (multilithed ed.), 207. See also *ibid.*, 99ff.

13. *Ibid.*, 405. See also *ibid.*, 222–23.

14. John Foster Dulles, Memorandum of May 18, 1950, Dulles Papers, I.G., 1950–54, Princeton University Library.

15. "Statement of Mr. Charles E. Bohlen Before the Voorhees

Group on 3 April 1950," Joseph M. Dodge Papers, Detroit Public Library.

16. Ellen J. Hammer, *The Struggle for Indochina* (Stanford, 1954), 270–72.

17. Jules Moch, *Histoire du Réarmament Allemand Depuis 1950* (Paris, 1965), 108–13, 125, 216; U.S. Senate, Committee on Foreign Relations, *Background Information Relating to Southeast Asia and Vietnam.* 89:1. Jan. 14, 1965 (Washington, 1965), 137; U.S. Agency for International Development, *U.S. Foreign Assistance . . . : Obligations and Loan Authorizations, July 1, 1945– June 30, 1961 (Revised)* (Washington, 1962), 12; Harry S Truman, *Memoirs* (Garden City, 1955), II, 519.

18. Dulles to Frank C. Laubach, Oct. 31, 1950, Dulles Papers.

19. U.S. Senate, Committee on Foreign Relations, *Hearings: United States Foreign Aid Programs in Europe.* 82:1 (Washington, 1951), 207. See also Christopher Emmett to Elmer Davis, March 26, 1951; Emmett to Paul Douglas, July 15, 1951; Memorandum of Dulles to Dean Acheson, Nov. 30, 1950, all in Dulles Papers.

20. U.S. Senate, Committee on Foreign Relations, *Foreign Aid Programs in Europe,* 207.

21. *Ibid.,* 208.

22. *Ibid.*

23. *Ibid.,* 211.

24. Allan B. Cole, *Conflict in Indochina and International Repercussions: A Documentary History, 1945–1955* (Ithaca, 1956), 171.

25. Dwight D. Eisenhower, *Mandate for Change* (Garden City, 1963), 333. Even by March 1951 French industrial interests complained to their Government about the activities of the various American missions in probing for possible access to raw materials. Their anxieties were justified the following September when the United States economic aid agreement signed directly with the Bao Dai regime pledged him to develop raw materials and semi-finished goods useful to the American stockpiling program and general needs. See Commission D'Enquête de la R.D.V. sur les Crimes de Guerre des Impérialistes Americains au Viet Nam, *Chronologie des*

Principaux Événements Relatifs aux Visées et Activities d'Agression des États-Unis au Viet Nam (Hanoi, 1967), 5–6. This manuscript cited hereafter as D.R.V., *Chronologie.*

26. Anthony Eden, *Full Circle* (Boston, 1960), 92.

27. Truman, *Memoirs,* II, 519. See also Eden, *Full Circle,* 92.

28. Eisenhower, *Mandate for Change,* 168. See also Gardner Patterson *et al., Survey of United States International Finance, 1953* (Princeton, 1954), 35n; Jacques Despuech, *Le Traffic de Piastres* (Paris, 1953), *passim.*

29. Eisenhower, *Mandate for Change,* 337.

30. *Ibid.,* 338.

31. Quoted in Alexander Werth, "Showdown in Viet Nam," *New Statesman and Nation,* April 8, 1950, 397. See also H. Navarre, *Agonie de l'Indochine, 1953–1954* (Paris, 1956), *passim;* Jean Lacouture and Philippe Devillers, *La Fin d'une Guerre: Indochine 1954* (Paris, 1960), 41–42; Hammer, *Struggle for Indochina,* 313–14; Eisenhower, *Mandate for Change,* 169, 338; Alexander Werth, *France, 1940–1955* (New York, 1956), 642–44.

32. "Speech Before the Council on Foreign Relations," Jan. 12, 1954. State Department Press Release No. 8, 4.

33. Eden, *Full Circle,* 100.

34. Eisenhower, *Mandate for Change,* 345.

35. Eden, *Full Circle,* 102.

36. Department of State, *American Foreign Policy, 1950–1955* (Washington, 1957), II, 2374ff., 2380.

37. Cole, *Conflict in Indochina,* 174.

38. Eisenhower, *Mandate for Change,* 346–47; Eden, *Full Circle,* 103.

39. U.K., *Documents Relating to British Involvement,* 66–67.

40. Department of State, *American Foreign Policy,* II, 2385. See also Lacouture and Devillers, *La Fin d'une Guerre,* 278–79; Department of State, *American Foreign Policy,* II, 2386.

41. Department of State, *American Foreign Policy,* II, 2389–90.

42. *NYT,* June 27, 1954, p. 1E.

43. Eden, *Full Circle,* 149. See also Franklin B. Weinstein, *Vietnam's Unheld Elections: The Failure to Carry Out the 1956 Re-*

unification Elections and the Effect on Hanoi's Present Outlook (Ithaca, Southeast Asia Program, 1966), 4–9; *NYT,* June 27, 1954, for the best accounts.

44. U.S. Senate, Committee on Foreign Relations, *Background Information,* 35. See also *ibid., 28–42.*

45. *Ibid., 58–59.*

46. *Ibid., 59.*

47. Eisenhower, *Mandate for Change,* 337–38.

48. *Ibid., 372.*

49. U.S. Senate, Committee on Foreign Relations, *Background Information,* 60.

50. *Ibid.*

51. *Ibid., 60–61.*

52. *Wall Street Journal,* July 23, 1954.

53. U.S. Senate, Committee on Foreign Relations, *Hearings: The Southeast Asia Collective Defense Treaty.* 83:2. Nov. 11, 1954 (Washington, 1954), 1.

54. U.S. Senate, Committee on Foreign Relations, *Background Information,* 63.

55. Department of State, *American Foreign Policy,* II, 2404; see also Department of State, *The Legality of U.S. Participation in the Defense of Viet-Nam* (Washington, March 1966), 10; Agency for International Development, *U.S. Foreign Assistance,* 40.

56. Cole, *Conflict in Indochina,* 226–27.

57. Quoted in Weinstein, *Vietnam's Unheld Election,* 33.

58. *Ibid.,* 33–37; Lacouture and Devillers, *La Fin d'une Guerre,* 301.

59. U.K., *Documents Relating to British Involvement,* 95. See also *ibid.,* 115–20; Weinstein, *Vietnam's Unheld Elections,* 47–49.

60. U.K., *Documents Relating to British Involvement,* 97–98; D.R.V., Ministry of Foreign Affairs, *Imperialist Schemes in Vietnam Against Peace and Reunification* (Hanoi, July 1958), 77–79; Weinstein, *Vietnam's Unheld Elections,* 53.

61. Department of State, *American Foreign Policy: Current Documents, 1956* (Washington, 1959), 861–62.

62. Quoted in Robert Scheer, *How the United States Got In-*

volved in Vietnam (Santa Barbara, 1965), 40. See also Nguyen Kien, *Le Sud-Vietnam Depuis Dien-Bien-Phu* (Paris, 1963), 109; Jean Lacouture, *Le Vietnam Entre Deux Paix* (Paris, 1965), 46; Z, "The War in Vietnam," *New Republic,* March 12, 1962, 24. Given the inherently decentralized character of repression, and the fact that executors do not issue statistics, estimates are by their nature approximate. The data cited in the text above are minimal, but the D.R.V., in *Chronologie,* 32, claim Diem's regime executed 77,500 persons from Geneva until the end of 1960. The I.C.C. reports tend to reinforce this estimate as entirely plausible, certainly if the repression of the religious sects is taken into account.

63. Gettleman, *Vietnam,* 166–79; D.R.V., *Imperialist Schemes,* 30ff.

64. Lacouture and Devillers, *La Fin d'une Guerre,* 301–02: Kien, *Sud-Vietnam,* 122–30; Lê Châu, *Le Révolution Paysanne du Sud Viet-Nam* (Paris, 1966), 16–24, 54–79.

65. U.S. Senate, Committee on Foreign Relations, *Background Information,* 75. See also Kien, *Sud-Vietnam,* 131; John D. Montgomery, *The Politics of Foreign Aid* (New York, 1962), 67–94; Fall, *Two Viet-Nams,* 303–06.

66. Gettleman, *Vietnam,* 256–57. See also Fall, *Two Viet-Nams,* 344; Devillers in Gettleman, *Vietnam,* 210ff.; Lacouture, *Vietnam,* 34ff.; Z, "The War in Vietnam," 21–26; James Alexander, "Deadlock in Vietnam," *Progressive,* Sept. 1962, 20–24; and especially George McT. Kahin and John W. Lewis, *The United States in Vietnam* (New York, 1967), chap. v, to cite only a few substantiating sources.

67. U.S. Senate, Committee on Foreign Relations, *Background Information,* 137; *NYT,* Dec. 1, 1965; *New York Herald Tribune,* Oct. 17, 1966.

68. D.R.V., Ministère des Affaires Étrangeres, *Memorandum.* . . . (Hanoi, Fevrier 1962), 33; see also U.S. Senate, Committee on Foreign Relations, *Background Information,* 76–78.

69. *Wall Street Journal,* Nov. 8, 1961.

70. U.S. Senate, Committee on Foreign Relations, *Background Information,* 81. See also *NYT,* Dec. 13, 1961.

71. U.S. Senate, Committee on Foreign Relations, *Background Information*, 83.

72. Lacouture, *Vietnam*, 56–57.

73. Department of State, *A Threat to the Peace: North Viet-Nam's Effort to Conquer South-Vietnam* (Washington, December 1961), Part I, 9.

74. *Ibid.*, Part II, 5.

75. *Ibid.*, Part I, 52; *NYT*, Nov. 27, 1961.

76. *NYT*, April 19, 1962.

77. U.S. Senate, Committee on Foreign Relations, *Background Information*, 88–89.

78. U.S. Senate, Committee on Foreign Relations, *Viet Nam and Southeast Asia*. 88:1 ["Mansfield Report"]. Jan. 1963 (Washington, 1963), 5.

79. *Ibid.*

80. U.S. Senate, Committee on Armed Services, *Hearings: Military Procurement Authorization, Fiscal Year 1964*. 88:1 (Washington, 1963), 707.

81. U.S. Senate, Committee on Foreign Relations, *Background Information*, 101. See also *NYT*, April 27, July 23, Sept. 9, 21, 1963.

82. *NYT*, Sept. 13, 1963.

83. Franz Schurmann, Peter Dale Scott, and Reginald Zelnik, *The Politics of Escalation in Vietnam* (New York and Boston, 1966), 23–25; *NYT*, Oct. 3, 1963; U.S. Senate, Committee on Foreign Relations, *Background Information*, 102.

84. *NYT*, Nov. 9, 1963.

85. *NYT*, Dec. 23, 1963. See also *NYT*, Nov. 29, Dec. 10, 14, 15, 20, 1963.

86. U.S. Senate, Committee on Foreign Relations, *Background Information*, 106–07.

87. *NYT*, March 6, 1964. See also *NYT*, Feb. 23, 1964; Schurmann *et al.*, *Politics of Escalation*, 27–34.

88. U.S. Senate, Committee on Foreign Relations, *Background Information*, 111–17.

89. U.S. Senate, Committee on Foreign Relations, *Background Information*, 124.

90. *NYT,* August 6, 1964. See also *Le Monde,* ed. hebd., Aug. 6–12, 1964.

91. *NYT,* August 11, 14, Sept. 25, 1964. See also Schurmann *et al., Politics of Escalation,* 35–43; D.R.V., Ministry of Foreign Affairs, *Memorandum Regarding the U.S. War Acts . . . of August 1964* (Hanoi, Sept. 1964), *passim;* U.S. Senate, Committee on Foreign Relations, *Hearings: The Gulf of Tonkin, The 1964 Incidents.* 90:2 (Washington, 1968), *passim.*

92. *NYT,* Nov. 2, 1964. See also *NYT,* August 25, 27, 28, Sept. 4, 1964.

93. *NYT,* Jan. 19, Feb. 3, 8, 10, 12, 13, 1965; Schurmann *et al., Politics of Escalation,* 44–61.

94. *NYT,* Feb. 18, 1965; see also *NYT,* Feb. 26, 1965.

95. The text is in Gettleman, *Vietnam,* 284–316. See also the answer by I. F. Stone in *ibid.,* 317–23.

96. *NYT,* March 12, 1965. See also *NYT,* March 1, 3, 28, 1965.

97. *NYT,* April 8, 1965.

98. *NYT,* April 8, 1965. See also *NYT,* March 26, April 3, 7, 1965.

99. See also Schurmann *et al., Politics of Escalation, passim.*

100. *NYT,* July 29, 1965.

101. Department of State, *The Heart of the Problem . . . Secretary Rusk, General Taylor Review Viet-Nam Policy in Senate Hearings* (Washington, March 1966), 12–13. See also Department of State, *Why Vietnam?* (Washington, August 20, 1965), 9ff.

102. George W. Ball, *The Issue in Viet-Nam* (Washington, March 1966), 18.

INDEX

Acheson, Dean: 41, 95, 100, 101
Adams, Brooks: 28
Adams, Henry: 28
Aerospace firms: 32
Africa: 50, 56
Agency for International Development: 71–73
Agricultural exports: 57
Air Force Association: 32
Alliance for Progress: 71, 81
Aluminum Corporation: 76
Arms producers: and military establishment, 31–32
Army Industrial College: 31
Association of the U.S. Army: 32–33

B-36 bomber: 32, 39
Baldwin, Hanson: 36, 124, 125
Ball, George: 131
Bao Dai: 94, 95, 97, 98, 101, 108
Bauxite: 53
Bethlehem Steel: 81
Bidault, Georges: 101
Bidwell, Percy W.: quoted, 79
Black, Eugene: 79, 129
Bogotá Conference: 67

Bohlen, Charles E.: 96–97
Bolivia: 53
Bombing: of D.R.V., 126–131
Bradley, Omar N.: 35, 39
Brazil: 53, 81
Brookings Institution: 141–142
Brown Brothers: 19
Bruce, David: 98, 99
Buenos Aires Conference, 1957: 67
Bureaucracy: xii; power of, 5; function of, 13
Business: and power, 9; and government posts, 19–20; and government leadership, 23–26; and military establishment, 30–33; hiring of retired officers, 33

Cabot, John M.: 23
Cahill, Gordon, Zachry & Riendel: 19
Caracas Conference, 1954: 67
Carter, Ledyard & Milburn: 19
Chiang Kai-shek: 95
Chile: 53
China: 53
Chromium: 53

Churchill, Winston: 104
CIA: 22, 29, 69
Civil disobedience: 134
Civilian authority: xiii–xiv, 27–47
Civilians: and military establishment, 43–47
Classes: in U.S. society, 9
Clayton, William L.: 23
Coffee: 67–68
Cold War: 28
Colgate-Palmolive: 76
Collado, Emilio G.: 73
Commodity agreements: 65–68, 80
Common Market nations: and exports, 56
Congo: 53
Consensus: xii–xiii, 133; limits of, 7–13
Copper: 53
Corn Products: 76
Coudert Brothers: 19
Counterpart funds: 69–70
Cuba: 29, 53, 82

Defense establishment: reorganizations of, 44–47
Defense Reorganization Act: of 1953, 44; of 1958, 45
De Gaulle, Charles: 91, 92, 127
Democratic Republic of Vietnam (D.R.V.): 110; bombing of, 126–131
Denfeld, Louis E.: 39
Detroit Bank: 19
Developing nations: and raw materials, 50–55; and export trade, 55–56; and world trade, 59–62; and stability, 78
Diem. See Ngo Dinh Diem
Diem regime: 110, 111, 112, 113–116, 117, 122, 123
Dillon, Douglas: 78
Dillon, Read & Co.: 19, 22
Diplomats: education of, 14–15

Dodge, Joseph M.: 19
Dollar crisis. See Gold crisis
Dominican Republic: 86
"Domino" theory: 85, 89, 98–99, 120, 124
Dong. See Pham Van Dong
Dulles, John Foster: 96, 97, 98, 101, 102, 103, 104, 105, 107, 109, 110, 111, 113; career origin of, 22; on foreign aid, 65; on nationalization, 81–82

Economic power. See Power
Eden, Anthony: 100, 107; quoted, 102–103
Education: of diplomats, 14–15
Eisenhower, Dwight D.: 34, 37, 40, 43, 45, 99, 100, 104, 109; quoted, 63, 108–109, 116
Eisenhower administration: xv
Europe: and U.S., xvi–xvii; U.S. investments in, 74–75; economic conflict with, 89
Export-Import Bank: 25, 64, 65, 71
Exports: U.S. and world, 55–58

Fair Deal: 47
Fairless Committee: 71
Food for Peace: 72
Ford Motor Company: 46
Foreign aid program: 68, 77
Foreign Assistance Act of 1948. See Marshall Plan
Forrestal, James: 22; quoted, 49
France: 74; and Vietnam, 91–102
Freedom: 8, 135

Gabon: 53
Gallagher, John: on imperialism, 83–84
GATT tariff: xvii, 63
Gavin, James M.: 32
Geneva agreement: 106–109

Geneva Conference, 1954: 102–105
Germany: 74
Gold crisis: xvi, xvii
Goldwater, Barry: 32
Gordon, Lincoln: 71
Goulart, President: 81
Gracey, Major-General: 93
Great Society: 47
Greece: 29, 86
Guyana: 53

H-bomb: 35, 41
Halberstam, David: 123
Hanna Mining: 81
Harriman, Averell: 19
Harriman family: 4
Hartz, Louis: 9
Ho Chi Minh: 92, 93, 103, 105, 108, 109, 112, 120
Hoffman, Paul G.: quoted, 50
Hoover, Herbert: 40
Hull, Cordell: 23
Humphrey, George M.: quoted, 78–79
Huntington, Samuel P.: 33, 34

Imperialism: 48, 83–84; and loans, 71
India: 53, 64
Indo-China: 90–93
Indonesia: 29, 53, 81
Institute for Defense Analysis: 46
International Control Commission: 114
International Trade Organization: 62, 67
Intervention: and U.S. foreign economic policy, 81–82
Investments abroad: U.S., and trade, 73–78; size of U.S., 74; profits on, 75–77
Iran: 29
Iron ore: 53
Italy: 74

Ivy League schools: and diplomats, 14–15

Japanese Matsumoto Mission: 129
Jessup, Philip: 95
Jessup Committee: 96
Johnson, Louis: 36, 39, 41, 42
Johnson, Lyndon: 81, 123, 125, 129; Johns Hopkins speech, 129–130
Johnson administration: 14

Kennan, George: 41, 42
Kennedy, John F.: 43; on foreign aid, 70; and Vietnam, 118, 122
Kennedy, Robert: 134
Kennedy administration: 36, 46, 65, 71
Khanh regime: 124, 126
Korean War: 41, 65
Kosygin, Premier: 127
Krock, Arthur: 127

Land reform: 79; in Vietnam, 115
Lasswell, Harold D.: 29, 30
Latin America: 53, 61, 66, 85; and exports, 56; and coffee, 67–68; and loans, 72; U.S. investment in, 75; investments in, 77; and land reform, 79; "free trade" area, 80
Lawyers: and government posts, 19
Lead: 53
LeClerc, General: 102
Left politics: 11
Life magazine: 113–114
Lilienthal, David: 41
Loans: 70–73
Lodge, Henry Cabot: 98

MacArthur, Douglas: controversy of 1951, 34
McCarthy, Eugene: 134
McKinley, William: 40
McNamara, Robert: 46, 47, 124, 125, 129, 131

McNamara-Bundy Plan: 128
Maddox: 125
Mahan, Alfred T.: 34
Malaya: 53
Manganese: 53; and U.S.-India relations, 64–65
Marshall, George C.: 94
Marshall Plan: 64, 70
Mass culture: 12
Mathews, Francis: 36
Mendès-France, Pierre: 106
Men Who Govern: 141–142
Military: "civilianized," 43–47
Military authority: in U.S., 27–47
Military establishment: 27; and business, 30–33; and arms producers, 31–32; extremes of viewpoint in, 35–36; and reactionaries, 36; after World War II, 37–43; and Vietnam, 90
Military ethic: 33–37
Military-industrial complex: xiii–xiv
Mills, C. Wright: 14, 15, 16, 19, 27, 29, 30, 33; quoted, 43–44
Missile program: 45–46
Le Monde: 125

National Security Council: 40, 41, 44
Navy League: 32
Nehru, Jawaharlal: 110
Neo-Hamiltonianism: 34
New Caledonia: 53
New Left: 134, 135
New York Times: 106, 123, 124, 126, 127, 128
Ngo Dinh Diem: 98
Ngo Dinh Nhu: 116
Nickel: 53
Nixon, Richard: 99–100, 104

Occupations: of individuals with posts in government, 1944–1960, 18, 20–21

Oil industry. *See* Petroleum
Operation Sunrise: 120–121

Peru: 53
Petroleum: industry and Dept. of the Interior, 25; U.S. control of industry, 74; profit on investment in, 76
Pfizer: 76
Pham Van Dong: 106, 110, 112, 119
Philippines: 80
Point Four program: 64, 65
Political power. *See* Power
Potsdam Conference: and Indo-China, 91
Power: men of, 3–26; and bureaucracies, 6; economic and political, 6; and business, 9; class opposition to, 10; and consensus, 11–12; world economic and U.S., 48–87; limitation of U.S., 138
Protest, social: 135–136
Public opinion. *See* Consensus
Puerto Rico: 80

Raborn, William F., Jr.: 22
Radicalism: and reason, 133–138
Ramo-Wooldridge Corporation: 45–46
Rand Corporation: 45
Raw materials: and U.S., 50–55; sources of U.S., 53; imports of, 54; stockpiling program, 65
Reason: and radicalism, 133–138
Resources for the Future: survey of raw materials, 51–52
Rhodesia: 53
Ridgway, Matthew B.: 35
Robertson, Walter S.: 113, 114
Robinson, Ronald: on imperialism, 83–84
Roosevelt, Franklin D.: 14, 31, 90
Roosevelt, Theodore: 28, 40
Rulers: versatility of, 13–23

Rusk, Dean: 118, 123, 131; quoted, 119–120, 121
Russia. *See* Soviet Union

Shoup, David M.: 35, 122
Smith, Walter Bedell: 103; quoted, 109
South Africa: 53
Southeast Asia Treaty Organization: 107, 109
Soviet Union: 53
Spanish-American War: 28
Stability: price of, and U.S., 78–83
Staley, Eugene: 119
Staley Plan: 120–121
Standard Oil of New Jersey: 73
Sugar: 63
Sukarno: 81
Sullivan & Cromwell: 17–19, 22
Symington, W. Stuart: 39
Synthetics: 52

Tariffs: and U.S., 62–68
Taylor, Maxwell D.: 35, 119, 129
TFX plane: 32
Thailand: 53
Thant: 125, 127
Third World. *See* Developing nations
Tin: 53
Trade. *See* World trade
Truman, Harry: 38, 39, 41, 97
Truman administration: 35; and Vietnam, 96–97
Tungsten: 53

Underdeveloped nations. *See* Developing nations
United Nations Conference on Trade and Development, Geneva, 1964: 80
United States: foreign policy and Vietnam War, xi–xii; and world economic power, xiv–xv, 48–87; and Europe, xvi–xvii; power in, 3–26; class structure of, 9; foreign policy decision makers, 1944–1960, 18; civilian authority in, 27–47; military authority in, 27–47; and raw materials, 50–55; imports of, 51; and world exports, 55–58; share in world exports and production of agricultural products, 58; and tariffs, 62–68; and commodity agreements, 65–68; expansion of agricultural exports, 68–70; loan program, 70–73; investment and trade, 73–78; investments abroad, size of, 74; profits on investments, 75–77; and stability, 78–83; foreign economic policy and direct intervention, 81–82; theory of global role, 83–87; in Vietnam, 1944–66, 88–132; and Vietnam, 1946–1949, 93–96; and Vietnam, 1950–53, 96–102; and French in Vietnam, 96–102; and Geneva Conference, 102–105; and Geneva agreement, 106–109; and Vietnam, 1955–59, 109–116; and Vietnam, 1959–64, 117, 126; and responsibility in Vietnam, 131–132
U.S. Defense Dept.: 41
U.S. Dept. of Commerce: Business and Defense Services Administration, 25
U.S. Dept. of the Interior: and petroleum industry, 25
U.S. Foreign Service: education of members of, 14–15
U.S. government: occupational origin of individuals with posts in, 1944–1960, 18; career origin of individuals in key positions, 1944–1960, 20–21; and business, 23–26; Brookings Institution report on men in, 141–142

U.S. Senate: Committee on Foreign Relations, 121
U.S. State Department: and H-bomb, 35
Universal Military Training: 38

Venezuela: 53
Vietnam: military undertaking in, xv; and imperialism, 85; land reform in, 115; bombing of, 126–131; U.S. responsibility in, 131–132
Vietnam War: U.S. foreign policy, xi–xii; and cost of, xv–xvi; history of, 88–132; 1946–1949, 93–96; 1950–1953, 96–102; Geneva Conference, 102–105; Geneva agreement, 106–109; 1955–1959, 109–116; 1959–1964, 117–126

Walker, Gen.: 36
Wall Street Journal: 109, 119
Warner, W. Lloyd: 16
Wealth: inequitable distribution of, 9
Weapons System Evaluation Group: 46
Weber, Max: 5
White Paper: Dec. 1961, 120; 1965, 128
Wilson, Woodrow: 23, 40
World Bank: 25, 71
World Trade: and world misery, 58–62; and developing nations, 59–62

Yale & Towne: 76
Yalta Conference: 91

Zinc: 53